I0152148

DEPARTMENT OF THE ARMY HISTORICAL SUMMARY

DEPARTMENT OF THE ARMY HISTORICAL SUMMARY

FISCAL YEAR 1971

COMPILED AND EDITED

BY

WILLIAM GARDNER BELL

GOVERNMENT REPRINTS PRESS
Washington, D.C.

© Ross & Perry, Inc. 2001 All rights reserved.

No claim to U.S. government work contained throughout this book.

Protected under the Berne Convention. Published 2001

Printed in The United States of America

Ross & Perry, Inc. Publishers
216 G Street, N.E
Washington, D.C. 20002
Telephone (202) 675-8300
Facsimile (202) 675-8400
info@RossPerry.com

SAN 253-8555

Government Reprints Press Edition 2001

Government Reprints Press is an Imprint of Ross & Perry, Inc.

Library of Congress Control Number: 2001096860
http://www.GPOreprints.com

ISBN 1-931839-34-4

⊗ The paper used in this publication meets the requirements for permanence established by the American National Standard for Information Sciences "Permanence of Paper for Printed Library Materials" (ANSI Z39.48-1984).

All rights reserved. No copyrighted part of this publication may be reproduced, stored in a retrieval system, or transmitted, in any form or by any means, electronic, photocopying, recording, or otherwise, without the prior written permission of the publisher.

Foreword

This document is a continuation, under a new title, of the United States Army's long-standing series of periodic reports, one published with only minor modifications of frequency and continuity since 1822. Until 1949 it was the Secretary of War's report of stewardship. From 1949 to 1968 it served as the Secretary of the Army's report and appeared with those of the other service secretaries in the Annual Report of the Department of Defense.

In May 1972, the consolidated report was canceled by the Secretary of Defense. To preserve its traditional and valuable reference document, the Army has published three reports—1969, 1970, 1971—that were in suspense, and will continue publication on a current basis. Effective with the 1969 edition, the title was changed from *Annual Report of the Secretary of the Army* to *Department of the Army Historical Summary*. The report will be prepared and published by the Chief of Military History and will continue to appear on a fiscal year schedule.

Washington, D.C.
1 February 1973

JAMES L. COLLINS, JR.
Brigadier General, USA
Chief of Military History

Contents

Illustrations

Illustrations are from Department of the Army files.

I. Introduction

During fiscal year 1971, with combat operations in Vietnam drastically reduced, American casualties at their lowest in five years, Vietnamization moving ahead, a large-scale troop redeployment in progress, and over-all strength declining to peacetime levels, the dimensions of a new Army challenge began to emerge. How could the Army, on the heels of an unpopular war, in the face of antimilitary sentiment and social ferment, with reduced strength and appropriations, and without resort to the draft, maintain a strong, viable, and professional ground force to meet its current and future roles and missions?

The changing conditions and prospects were evidenced in many ways. A key factor was the gradual and appreciable withdrawal from a combat to a holding and support role in Vietnam coincident with the redeployment of large numbers of troops and units from the war zone.

Battle casualties also decreased markedly from the preceding year's levels: 2,135 soldiers were killed and 15,488 wounded in the twelve-month period, compared with 4,672 and 34,826 respectively in 1970. More than half the wounded—7,789—were returned to duty without requiring hospitalization. Total Army battle casualties of the war—January 1, 1961, to June 30, 1971—were 30,173 killed and 199,142 wounded. Another 275 men were missing in action as the year closed, 62 of whom were known to have been captured.

U.S. Army major unit strength in Vietnam was reduced during the year by $3\frac{2}{3}$ division force equivalents, leaving only $2\frac{1}{3}$ equivalents at year's end, a reduction of 6 division forces from the wartime peak. By June 30, 1971, less than 200,000 American soldiers remained in Vietnam, about 162,000 below the wartime high.

Over-all U.S. Army strength dropped correspondingly, from the wartime peak of 1,570,000 reached in June 1968 to the 1,124,000 level of June 30, 1971—a total reduction of about 446,000 over the three-year period.

In the coming year the Army will continue to redeploy forces from Vietnam, reduce over-all strength, redistribute equipment and personnel, meet commitments elsewhere in the world, and maintain authorized strength while moving toward a zero draft. The transition to a volunteer force naturally raised problems and absorbed an increasing amount of attention during the past year.

Many considerations are involved in the concept of an all-volunteer

Hon. Stanley R. Resor
Secretary of the Army
July 1965 - July 1971

U.S. Army and in America's ability and inclination to sustain one. The statesmen who framed the constitution propounded a democratic philosophy against large standing armies in peacetime and set the directions of a military policy under which the citizen soldier would be called to the colors in times of emergency to fight the nation's wars. The principle served well enough until the middle of the twentieth century, when the United States, emerging from World War II as a major world power, could no longer demobilize and return to a small professional Army. Adequate preparedness now required peacetime military forces at levels above citizen inclinations for voluntary service, and in 1948 the nation turned to peacetime conscription.

As the United States moves into the eighth decade of the century, more than half of its citizens are under thirty years of age and view the draft, operative throughout their lifetime, as a normal state of affairs. Yet limited call-ups and highly selective eligibility and deferment, along with the heavy involvement of draftees in the Vietnam War and the traditional discontent of a free people with compulsory military service (especially in peacetime or under conditions of limited or undeclared war), brought the draft into question and inspired broad official and private interest in developing a more acceptable procedure.

Thus on March 27, 1969, the President of the United States created the Commission on an All-Volunteer Armed Force, chaired by former Secretary of Defense Thomas S. Gates, Jr., to "develop a comprehensive plan for eliminating conscription and moving toward an all-volunteer armed force." In its report of February 20, 1970, the commission agreed unanimously "that the nation's interests will be better

Hon. Robert F. Froehlke
Secretary of the Army
Appointed July 1971

served by an all-volunteer force, supported by an effective stand-by draft, than by a mixed force of volunteers and conscripts." Two months later, on April 23, 1970, the President in a message to the Ninety-first Congress proposed that the nation "begin moving toward an end of the draft and its replacement with an all-volunteer armed force," while reforming the draft system along more equitable lines. Congress responded with actions in both areas, notably a lottery system for draft eligibility and proposals for substantial pay increases for personnel entering military service.

In response to the Commander in Chief's direction to move toward a volunteer force and the Secretary of Defense's zero-draft target date of July 1, 1973, the Army launched a broad range of actions to move to the new footing: actions calculated to sustain and elevate the professional environment, provide a better life for military personnel, and inspire public esteem for the men and women who serve the nation. The underlying principle was that the Army be disciplined, highly motivated, and thoroughly professional. These conditions are by no means unattainable. For despite the problems that face the armed forces today and the difficulties that lie ahead, the Army has a proud record of achievement and a wealth of dedicated and able professionals to sustain it.

With the end of the Vietnam War in view and the broad lines of peacetime adjustment and future operation taking shape, the incumbent Secretary of the Army, Stanley R. Resor, completed six years of Army stewardship and, on June 30, 1971, passed the reins to his successor. Robert F. Froehlke, Assistant Secretary of Defense for Administration, became Secretary of the Army on July 1, 1971.

II. Operational Forces

Operational forces are those elements of a nation's military resources that carry out strategic, tactical, and administrative missions—offensive and defensive—in support of national objectives. The operational area embraces organization, deployment, readiness, mobility, communications, and air and civil defense, along with a variety of other functions and processes that contribute to the general goals.

In fiscal year 1971 the Army pursued its most rapid demobilization since the end of World War II. The active Army force structure was reduced from 17⅓ to 13⅔ divisions—2⅔ divisions less than before Vietnam. There were 5⅔ divisions in the continental United States and Hawaii, 1 in Korea, 2⅔ divisions in Vietnam, and 4⅓ in Europe. Special mission forces continued on station in Berlin, Panama, and Alaska. The active Army's total military strength dropped from 1,511,000 at the end of fiscal year 1969 to 1,124,000 at the close of fiscal year 1971. The forecast is for about 892,000 by the end of the coming fiscal year. The reductions reflect diminished military requirements in Vietnam and elsewhere; savings in operating funds will be applied to essential research and development, modernization of forces, training improvements, and career attractiveness.

National military strategy requires the Army to maintain peacetime general purpose forces adequate to meet simultaneously a major Communist attack in either Europe or Asia while helping allies deal with other threats and while contending with minor contingencies elsewhere. During the past year fiscal constraints have required the Army to develop austere programs to meet this requirement while continuing its role in Vietnam and assisting allies in developing their defensive capabilities. Because of these constraints the Army has had to make adjustments between force structure and modernization. Plans call for a smaller, tougher, high quality Army capable of performing its mission.

The Pacific and the Far East [1]

The major withdrawal of U.S. forces from Vietnam served as a basis for the reorganization of U.S. military region command structures in that country. Accordingly, the headquarters of II Field Force was returned to Fort Hood, Texas, and inactivated on May 3, 1971, being replaced by the Third Regional Assistance Group. At the same time, the Delta Regional Assistance Command replaced the Delta Military

---

[1] See chapter 3 for the details on the Vietnam War.

Assistance Command as the senior U.S. headquarters in Military Region 4. I Field Force was reorganized and redesignated the Second Regional Assistance Group on May 16, 1971. On the same day, Headquarters, United States Army Forces, Military Region 2, was established to provide operational control over U.S. Army units in the region. This headquarters was under the operational control of the Second Regional Assistance Group, while units in Military Region 3 were under the Third Regional Assistance Group. In addition to achieving an over-all reduction in military strength, these reorganizations facilitated the continuation of the redeployment program and the disposition of military equipment.

In addition to the redeployments from Vietnam, U.S. forces in Korea were reduced by 18,403 spaces by the withdrawal and inactivation of the 7th Infantry Division. The remaining U.S. major unit, the 2d Infantry Division, was replaced along the demilitarized zone (except for a 500-meter strip astride the access to Panmunjom) by a Korean division, and moved to a reserve position. This reduction and repositioning of U.S. Army units will not significantly alter the relative military balance between North and South Korea. The latter has shown increasing skill in coping with North Korean infiltration efforts. South Korea's military position will be further strengthened under comprehensive modernization assistance to be provided by the United States over the next five years.

There were considerable reductions in U.S. Army facilities in Japan during the year, due primarily to diminishing support requirements in Southeast Asia. Fifteen logistical-type facilities were transferred to other services or released to Japan. Headquarters, U.S. Army, Japan, remained at Camp Zama and, although operations were significantly reduced, continued to provide diverse logistical support to U.S. and allied forces in the Far East.

U.S. Army forces in Thailand were also reduced during the year as road construction tasks were completed and service support units could be consolidated.

Europe

The strategy and forces of the North Atlantic Treaty Organization (NATO) received searching review on both sides of the Atlantic in calendar year 1970. The United States participated in a NATO study on Alliance Defense Problems for the 1970s, which concluded that "the commitment of substantial North American forces deployed in Europe is essential both politically and militarily for effective deterrence and defense and to demonstrate the solidarity of NATO. Their replacement by European forces would be no substitute. At the same time their significance is closely related to an improved European defense effort."

President Richard M. Nixon's message to the North Atlantic council in December 1970 stated: "We have agreed that NATO's conventional forces must not only be maintained, but in certain key areas, strengthened. Given a similar approach by our allies, the United States will maintain and improve its own forces in Europe and will not reduce them unless there is reciprocal action from our adversaries." Army planning for Europe has been keyed to the President's pledge for nuclear as well as nonnuclear forces.

The Army maintains a powerful armored and mechanized nuclear-supported force which is the keystone of NATO's land defenses in central Europe. Major forces are 2 armored divisions, $2\frac{1}{3}$ mechanized infantry divisions, and 2 armored cavalry regiments. Supporting units include an effective group of nuclear-capable artillery units.

Major deployments to Europe during the year consisted of three Chaparral-Vulcan battalions. Two were assigned as divisional anti-aircraft artillery battalions and the other was assigned to the 32d Army Air Defense Command, completing deployments to U.S. Army, Europe, of this type of unit.

Two major units were redesignated during the year. The 4th Armored Division became the 1st Armored Division and the 56th Artillery Group was redesignated the 56th Artillery Brigade. There were also changes in the logistical command and control and organizational structure, refining major modifications made last year. The position of Commanding General, Theater Army Support Command, was redesignated as a lieutenant general's billet. On March 11, 1971, the U.S. Army Medical Command, Europe, and the 15th Military Police Brigade were transferred from the control of the U.S. Army, Europe (USAREUR), and assigned as subordinate elements of the support command.

Planning continued on the development of a wartime line of communication in Europe. The operational project authorizing the prepositioning of port equipment was approved; bilateral negotiations continued with the United Kingdom, Belgium, and Luxembourg and were completed with the Netherlands; and requirements for the line of communication and port force were validated. Several unit activations were delayed by budget constraints and congressional reservations.

On August 6, 1970, the United States and Spain signed a five-year agreement authorizing continued U.S. use of four major military facilities in Spain. The U.S. Army was obligated to provide $21.1 million in Military Assistance Program (MAP) equipment and spare parts, and the MAP will fund up to $4.9 million for training over the length of the agreement. The United States also agreed to guarantee $120 million in credits, part of which will fund U.S. Army construction of a territorial command communications net for Spain.

Alaska and Latin America

U.S. Army, Alaska, the Army component of the unified Alaskan Command, continued to be responsible for ground defense in the northernmost state. Of its major forces, an infantry brigade was located at Fort Richardson near Anchorage, while another was at Fort Wainwright north of the Alaska Range. Each brigade had two infantry battalions and a battalion of artillery. Operations of these active Army forces and of Reserve Component forces in Alaska were closely integrated during the past year in order to increase combat capability without increasing costs or personnel.

In the Panama Canal Zone the commander of U.S. Army Forces, Southern Command, had an infantry brigade for ground defense, with one of its infantry battalions on the Atlantic side of the zone and the other plus a mechanized battalion on the Pacific side. Also on the Atlantic coast at Fort Gulick was a reduced-size Special Forces Group to support military assistance training in Latin America and act as a fourth defense battalion in emergencies. At Fort Sherman the Jungle Operations Training Center provided jungle training for command members as well as for personnel destined for Southeast Asia. And the School of the Americas continued to conduct training courses (in Spanish) for Latin American military personnel.

Continental United States

In line with the general reduction of forces and required realignments, Army air defense forces in the continental United States were reduced by twenty-four Nike-Hercules firing batteries and ten headquarters and headquarters batteries in fiscal year 1971. The Army Air Defense Command was restructured into two regional commands and a separate brigade for command and control functions.

Of the 24 batteries phased out of the force structure, 13 were manned by the active Army and 11 by the National Guard. Twenty-seven of the remaining 48 are manned by the Guard. Three active Army batteries in Alaska were inactivated. Under the reduction the Minneapolis–St. Paul defense area was eliminated, while the Seattle area was unaffected. The remaining eight defense regions were reduced by from 1 to 5 batteries each.

As the fiscal year closed, a realignment of Continental Army boundaries took effect that involved the consolidation of two headquarters and the transfer of some activities to a third. The Fourth and Fifth United States Armies were consolidated and their headquarters merged at Fort Sam Houston, Texas. The new headquarters, designated the Fifth U.S. Army, was made responsible for activities in fourteen states: Arkansas, Indiana, Illinois, Iowa, Kansas, Louisiana, Michigan, Minnesota, Missouri, Nebraska, New Mexico, Oklahoma, Texas, and Wisconsin. Army activities in Colorado, the Dakotas, and Wyoming were transferred to the Sixth U.S. Army at the Presidio of San Francisco, California. The consolidation enabled the Army to combine related functions and save on management overhead. Merger of the headquarters, to be effective July 1, 1971, eliminated 621 military and 609 civilian positions with anticipated annual savings of $11.4 million.

In another organizational development, one designed to insure the application of the latest technological advances to techniques and tactical requirements, the Army activated the 1st Cavalry Division (TRICAP) at Fort Hood, Texas, on May 5, 1971. TRICAP is an acronym for Triple Capable, reflecting the combination of armor, airmobile infantry, and air cavalry combat units within the division. The new division was organized from elements of the 1st Armored Division at Fort Hood and the colors of the 1st Air Cavalry Division redeployed from Vietnam. It replaced the 1st Armored Division in the Army force structure and left the III Corps at Fort Hood with two active Army divisions. The colors of the 1st Armored Division were sent to Europe where they replaced those of the 4th Armored Division, which reverted to inactive status.

The 1st Cavalry Division (TRICAP) is a 13,000-man force consisting of an armored brigade, an airmobile infantry brigade, and an air cavalry combat brigade. While the armored and airmobile infantry brigades are similar to those in other divisions, the air cavalry combat brigade is a new formation that combines the air cavalry squadron proven in Vietnam with a new air cavalry squadron in a highly mobile and flexible antitank force. The air cavalry combat brigade will ultimately be provided with attack helicopters equipped with the TOW antitank missile system.

This new division is the test foundation of the future Army. Its organization will be modified on the basis of extensive tests scheduled for the 1971–72 period.

Army Readiness

The personnel readiness of some continental U.S. units and the major oversea commands improved during fiscal year 1971. Intensified personnel management actions were taken to improve the 82d Airborne Division's readiness and to prepare Reforger units (those located in the United States but assigned to reinforcement missions in Europe using prepositioned equipment) for their annual exercises. In midyear a program was begun to improve the personnel status of units in U.S. Army, Europe, and by June readiness ratings there had been raised.

In U.S. Army, Pacific, meanwhile, redeployments from Vietnam and Korea had made it possible to improve the readiness of remaining units in U.S. Army, Pacific. Toward the end of the year, as the general reduction in Army strength progressed, certain units in the continental United States and the smaller oversea commands reported a decrease in personnel readiness. Unit personnel turnover rates in fiscal year 1971 were generally similar to those of 1970, with the single exception of the 82d Airborne Division, where turnover declined significantly.

Personnel shortages and turbulence, along with austere funding, precluded any substantial improvement in training readiness in fiscal year 1971. In some cases, commanders placed a number of subordinate elements in a standby status in order to conduct effective training within reduced operating strength. The standby elements received no unit training, resulting in a deficiency in planned capabilities. Personnel turnover frequently forced recycling of training at lower levels to insure basic proficiency in primary skills. Particularly in the continental United States, high personnel turnover adversely affected unit training.

Major commands were not able to conduct effective exercise programs in the year because of congressional reductions of $3.7 million in field exercise funds from the Army's operation and maintenance budget. Only in Exercise Reforger II was it possible for a full U.S. division to maneuver in the field.

The Army's logistic readiness improved worldwide almost continuously during fiscal year 1971. Special management techniques were used successfully in stateside and oversea commands to overcome unit and resource problems. Small temporary declines early in the year, particularly in the Continental Army Command, were due to unit conversions and reorganizations, personnel shortages, and funding constraints. By year's end, unit logistic readiness conditions had improved.

Strategic Mobility

The U.S. capability to deploy forces rapidly to any point in the world to support national strategy becomes increasingly important when forward deployed forces are reduced. Such a capability requires ready active and Reserve Component forces combined with airlift, sealift, and prepositioned materiel.

During the past year, controlled humidity storage in Europe for prepositioned equipment for reinforcing divisions and support forces moved ahead to about 50 percent completion. Field testing and production of the C–5A heavy logistic transport continued, with deployment capability expanding as planes entered the active fleet. The capability of the Civil Reserve Air Fleet was also enhanced by the introduction of the 747 aircraft into commercial airline operations.

The sealift capability continued to decline as the number of ships in the U.S. Merchant Marine fleet declined and with shipping undergoing a transition from break-bulk to container operations. In calendar year 1970 only thirteen oceangoing vessels were completed in U.S. yards, and of these, six were containerships and seven were tankers. Of equal importance is the fact that the Military Sealift Command's fleet of World War II ships is rapidly declining and is no longer capable of supporting the rapid deployment requirements of more recent times. The Army thus continued to support Department of Defense efforts to obtain, through a charter hire arrangement, ten multipurpose ships to transport the Army's wheeled and tracked vehicles and certain types of aircraft that are not self-deployable. The Army also continued to support programs that would insure that American transportation systems are utilized fully and effectively and that would improve the condition of the Merchant Marine.

Army Operations Center

As the Army's primary command and control hub, the Army Operations Center monitored such diverse matters as the crisis in Jordan, the Sky Marshal program to thwart the hijacking of commercial airliners, and the movement of chemical munitions from Army depots for dumping at sea. In a worldwide command post exercise in January-February 1971 the center provided command, control, and administrative facilities for the Army Staff. To make the center's operational system more effective, new equipment has been added and design and programing have been regularly modernized. The system is closely integrated with other Army automated data processing and reporting systems.

Military Support Operations

In May 1971, federal forces were employed to assist civil authorities during a civil disturbance for the first time since the riots that followed the murder of Dr. Martin Luther King in April 1968. Task Force Potomac and Task Force Military District of Washington (MDW) were deployed to Washington, D.C., on May 2, 1971, to assist police in countering plans by a group called the People's Coalition for Peace and Justice to disrupt traffic and deny access to federal government buildings during the period May 3–5. Federal forces were employed on Potomac River bridges, at key traffic circles, and at other locations to provide security and assist police. The disruptive tactics were unsuccessful, and Task Force Potomac was released on the afternoon of May 4 to return to home stations. Task Force MDW continued to provide security at key locations on May 4 and 5 and was released on May 6 to return to home stations. No confrontations occurred between demonstrators and federal forces during this civil disturbance.

Federal forces were not called upon to act in any other disturbance during fiscal year 1971, but they did respond to fifty-four requests for civil disturbance control equipment—protective masks, tear gas grenades, protective vests, and communications equipment—providing such items to civil law enforcement agencies and the National Guard in twelve states and the District of Columbia.

During the year a study was made of the Army's approach to civil disturbances. Policies and procedures, doctrine, organization and training, tactics and techniques, funding, support to civil authorities and the National Guard, and the potential threat through 1975 were examined, leading to 108 recommendations by the study groups for changes in civil disturbance policies, procedures, and equipment.

The Army also continued to support the Secret Service in its role of protecting the President and Vice President of the United States and the visiting heads of foreign states, providing explosive ordnance disposal personnel, helicopters, and other equipment and personnel. Requirements reached a peak in September and October 1970 during the twenty-fifth anniversary celebration at the United Nations and the congressional campaign.

The Army responded to a substantially larger number of requests for explosive ordnance disposal assistance concerning bomb scares, disarming of homemade bombs, transportation accidents involving explosives, and disposal of war souvenirs. Over 5,500 requests were acted upon during the year. In response to the increasing problem raised by the homemade bomb, civil authorities were trained in explosive ordnance reconnaissance, sabotage devices, and safety.

Project MAST (Military Assistance to Safety and Traffic) was undertaken with the participation of the Departments of Transportation, Health, Education, and Welfare, and Defense, to test the feasibility of using military helicopters in civil medical evacuation roles. The project created considerable public interest and support. Field tests were conducted from July 15 to December 31, 1970, at five locations: Fort Sam Houston, Texas; Fort Lewis, Washington; Fort Carson, Colorado; Luke Air Force Base, Arizona; and Mountain Home Air Force Base, Idaho. As the test period was closing, the Secretary of Defense authorized continued support at test sites pending report completion. Stanford Research Institute was awarded a contract to study the MAST concept and develop a cost analysis for use if the program is continued. During the test period 413 medical evacuations were made at the five test sites, for a total of 744 flying hours.

Under the President's program to provide federal resources to aid the District of Columbia government in combating crime, the Army assisted the Metropolitan Police Department in several ways. Technical assistance was provided to develop a viable police communications network, nine police officers were trained at Fort Wolters, Texas, as helicopter pilots, and helicopters were loaned to the police department for proficiency flying pending receipt of police craft and, during the May 1971 civil disturbances in Washington, for aerial command and control.

Army assistance to state and local authorities in natural disasters reached a peak in late February and early March 1971 as a result of flooding in Nebraska and severe weather in Oklahoma, Texas, Kansas, and North Carolina. More than 300 Army personnel participated in support operations. A total of 2,046 civilians were transported in Army aircraft as evacuees or for emergency medical treatment, and Army aircraft delivered 656 tons of hay and assorted supplies.

Military assistance in varying degrees was provided to state and local authorities to deal with drought, forest fires, and flash floods; to clear debris; and to alleviate utility failures temporarily. Help ranged from the assignment of two men and a tank truck to deal with a water shortage in a small community, to the commitment of 464 men with trucks, helicopters, generators, cots, blankets, and rations in the wake of Hurricane Celia in August 1970.

The Army also provided medical and other aid to foreign countries under emergency conditions in fiscal year 1971, notably in Jordan. The civil war there in September 1970 created a need for medical services that far exceeded Jordanian resources. On September 19, King Hussein addressed an urgent request to the U.S. Ambassador for assistance. The Army's 32d Surgical Hospital and the Air Force's 48th Air Transportable Hospital were deployed from Europe and established a joint facility in the new King Hussein Military Hospital in Amman. As the Jordanian hospital had no furnishings, electricity, or running water when the Americans arrived, tents were erected to house U.S. communications and power equipment, messing facilities, and motor pool, engineering, and carpentry shops. Water purification and laundry units were in continuous operation. In a full month of service, U.S. medical personnel treated 471 outpatients and performed 1,252 surgical operations. The facility had 191 admissions, 101 dispositions, and 90 beds occupied when the patients were turned over to the International Commission of the Red Cross on October 30, 1970. Most of the mobile hospital's equipment was turned over to the Jordanian government when the staff returned to Germany.

The Office of Civil Defense through the Agency for International Development offered one million pounds of Civil Defense fallout shelter food supplies to Dacca, East Pakistan, for relief of victims of the cyclone that struck low-lying areas along the Bay of Bengal in mid-November 1970, drowning hundreds of thousands of persons and displacing hundreds of thousands of survivors. The canned survival biscuits—normally intended as an emergency ration for public fallout shelters in case of enemy attack—were airlifted and distributed throughout the devastated area by the 182d U.S. Army Aviation Company (Assault Helicopter).

Psychological Operations

The bulk of psychological operations (PSYOP) programs and activities continued to be centered in Asia in 1971. Units located in Germany, Korea, Panama, Thailand, Okinawa, Japan, Taiwan, and South Vietnam participated in a wide variety of programs to support U.S. national objectives and third country programs and objectives.

As part of an Army PSYOP improvement program, a staff officer course was established at Fort Bragg, North Carolina, to supplement the basic officer course by concentrating on instruction in PSYOP functions and duties at the General Staff level.

During the fiscal year a substantial increase in PSYOP reserve forces was proposed; the increases were to be made in conjunction with reorganization of Reserve Component units in the coming fiscal year. Also begun during the year were preliminary tests of a PSYOP automated information system. Conducted by the 7th PSYOP Group on Okinawa, the system is designed to provide the user with information and data needed to make predictions and decisions on PSYOP planning and programing.

Special Forces and Special Action Forces

The decline in the over-all size of the active Special Forces that began in 1969 continued in fiscal year 1971. Active groups dropped from six to five, while elements were maintained in oversea areas such as Germany, Okinawa, Thailand, and the Canal Zone.

One of the more significant changes was the termination of the Civilian Irregular Defense Group program in Vietnam. In December 1970 the last of the remote camps that had been manned by indigenous local forces, Vietnamese Special Forces command personnel, and U.S. Special Forces advisers were turned over to the Vietnamese Ranger Command. In March 1971 the 5th Special Forces Group was reduced to a small color guard detachment and returned to Fort Bragg, its home station seven years before. The 6th Special Forces Group was inactivated, and the 5th Special Forces Group was reorganized using the assets and assuming the missions and orientation of the 6th Special Forces Group.

Modernization continued to be a major concern during the year, affected by limitations on the size of the Army in the postwar years and the success of new initiatives to create interest while improving the professional standards of Special Forces. One of these initiatives is a program called SPARTAN, Special Proficiency at Rugged Training and Nation-building. Its goal is to improve training within the constraint of limited funding, expand garrison support requirements, and enhance the motivation of today's young soldiers. The program is designed to maintain the proficiency of Special Forces soldiers through physically challenging work and emphasis on domestic actions akin to internal defense and development missions. As examples of both types of training, a 29-man detachment began retracing the 3,000-mile route through the American Northwest of the Lewis and Clark Expedition in the early years of the nineteenth century, while other detachments, at the invitation of local officials, have worked in communities near Fort Bragg to help those communities help themselves.

Military training team assistance to friendly foreign countries continued to be a major activity of Special Action Forces. Despite pressing personnel reductions, four of these organizations, each with a Special Forces Group as its nucleus, remained ready to respond to requests for U.S. advisory assistance from countries willing to help themselves. In Latin America, thirteen countries received assistance ranging from communications training in Honduras to a road survey in Panama.

Civil Affairs and Civic Action

The major civil affairs and civic action commitments and responsibilities in oversea areas remained in Southeast Asia. U.S. Army civil affairs units in the Canal Zone, Okinawa, and South Vietnam participated in a wide variety of advisory and operational activities designed to improve agriculture, education, roads, utilities systems, facilities of various kinds, and other activities to encourage host-country counterpart military forces to undertake enterprises that would promote the welfare of their people. The thirteen-man civic action team on Majuro Atoll in the Marshall Islands continued to participate in the program sponsored by the Department of the Interior in the Pacific trust territories.

The relocation of the U.S. Army Civil Affairs School, the only facility of its type in the Defense establishment, from Fort Gordon, Georgia, to Fort Bragg, North Carolina, was approved as the year closed. It will collocate related activities at the newly established Army Institute for Military Assistance.

Military Assistance

During the year the Army contributed in a major way to sustaining and improving the readiness posture of Free World military forces. In executing the Department of Defense program, the Army recognized the continuing trend toward reducing the dependence of foreign countries on direct military assistance in the form of grant aid. Some countries had made the transition from grant aid to become purchasers of military equipment and services such as training, and others were moving in that direction. The changeover was especially noticeable in Europe. However, there was a dramatic increase in funds provided for grant aid and in credits for foreign military sales, reflecting the continued concern for improving the defense capabilities of allied nations.

Greece, Turkey, and Spain remained dependent upon the United States for substantial funding to support their military programs. In Europe, burden-sharing was stressed as a means of spreading the cost of common defense. In Asia the objectives of Vietnamization were being fulfilled as Vietnam assumed a principal fighting role with U.S. forces in operations in Cambodia, Laos, and South Vietnam. The performance of Korean and Thai ground forces in Vietnam confirmed the soundness of U.S. military assistance policies and programs. The Army continued to study the Nixon Doctrine, in order to assess its military implications, and proposed legislation on security assistance. Application of the doctrine may mean an initial increase in the level of military assistance to offset a reduction in U.S. armed forces in the region, while the new legislation, when enacted, should provide a more comprehensive view of military assistance and related programs in the economic and humanitarian area and enable the Army to manage its part of such programs more effectively.

Grant aid for foreign military training by U.S. Army agencies amounted to $20.5 million. The Army received about $7.2 million for training that supported military sales to foreign customers. From the seventy-one countries represented in the Army instructional program, 18,666 students were trained in continental United States and oversea facilities through formal courses, orientation tours, and observer or on-the-job training. Seventy mobile training teams and sixty-seven field training service personnel were sent into various countries to train foreign personnel in military and technical subjects.

In addition to these Army programs, some 2,215 spaces in Army schools in the United States were allocated to the Air Force and Navy and to the Agency for International Development for foreign military students. Of this number, about 960 Vietnamese Air Force pilots took rotary-wing training under the Vietnamization program in special courses at the English Language School at Lackland Air Force Base and at Fort Wolters, Texas, and Fort Stewart, Georgia.

Communications and Electronics

The Army participated in two military satellite communications programs during the year: the Defense Satellite Communications System for the Defense Communications System and the Tactical Satellite Communications Program to support the Army's tactical communications requirements.

The Defense Satellite Communications System is currently operational using twenty-three drifting satellite repeaters and a complex of twenty-nine government-owned ground terminals operated by the three services. The Army operates fourteen of these terminals, including two heavy terminals at Fort Dix, New Jersey, and Camp Roberts, California. All terminals are being modified to provide increased capacity and to operate with a new type satellite, the first of which will be launched into a stationary orbit over the equator in November 1971.

All of the services participated in a tactical satellite communications feasibility testing program that was completed in June 1970. Under the program sixty-five advanced development model terminals were built in three sizes: manpacked, mounted in a $1/4$-ton truck, and mounted in the $1\frac{1}{4}$-ton truck. Designated as the Interim Operational Capability, these radio sets have been used to develop tactical satellite communications operating procedures, and during the fiscal year they supported such major maneuvers as Reforger II in Germany and Freedom Vault in Korea. Terminals were also sent to Yugoslavia to provide communications for President Nixon during his visit there.

The Army, in co-ordination with the Defense Communications Agency, the Joint Tactical Communications Office, and the Marine Corps, prepared and submitted as the year closed a draft Ground Mobile Forces Satellite Communications Development Concept paper that proposes an initial tactical satellite communications capability for the Army and the Marine Corps, to be operational in 1977. Three types of terminals similar to those described above would be developed and produced in quantity under the plan. The system would provide multichannel tactical satellite communications from the field army down through corps, division, and brigade echelons, and would provide high priority net radio (push-to-talk single channel) communications for key mobile users within the field army.

A new joint-services program called TRI-TAC was established during the year to fill the gap in tactical communications development caused by the discontinuation of Project Mallard, the international co-operative development program jointly sponsored by the United States, Australia, Canada, and the United Kingdom. In congressional consideration of the 1971 Defense budget, the Senate-House Conference Committee on Authorizations in September 1970 declined to authorize funds for Mallard, recommending that it be reoriented to give priority to U.S. requirements without the complication of active international participation. In October 1970 the United States announced its withdrawal, and all participants subsequently agreed that the project should be terminated. Co-operative development ceased in January 1971.

Following the action on the international side of the program, the Department of Defense established the Joint Tactical Communications (TRI–TAC) Program. The Army is responsible for administrative and logistic support of the new TRI–TAC office; the military manning level is to be supported on an equal basis among the U.S. military departments. The TRI–TAC program will provide communications equipment of various types for U.S. military forces, using existing tactical systems as starting points leading to common and interoperable systems by the 1980s. As the year closed, preparations were being made for the first TRI–TAC development, a new analog-digital tactical automatic switch. Although not yet formally given the task, the Army anticipates that it will be designated to develop the switch. As the program proceeds, all services will be assigned developmental responsibility for various TRI–TAC items. New equipment developed in the program will eventually replace that currently under procurement for unilateral Army tactical communications programs.

Under the Army's Electromagnetic Compatibility Program, modeling techniques, computer replication procedures, and analysis methods have been used to help the developers of secure communications for the Army of the future. By measuring the communicability of present and proposed links and applying the degrading effects of interference on these links, their susceptibility and vulnerability to interference—intentional or accidental—can be determined. The correlation between the band widths of proposed secure systems with existing secure and non-secure systems is a goal of the compatibility program. Study will reveal the impact on the frequency spectrum of all secure communications and evaluate the trade-offs that must be made, such as an increase in noise and a decrease in available frequency spectrum because of the larger band widths required for secure communications. Eventually, a practical compromise must be reached between secure system improvements and increases in band widths.

Civil Defense

Despite continuing efforts to achieve and maintain peace, nuclear attack on the United States is always a possibility. The Office of Civil Defense (OCD) is charged with carrying out the federal role in preparing citizens to cope with the effects of such an attack.

There is also a growing awareness that communities prepared to meet the effects of attack are better prepared to deal with peacetime hazards and disasters. The nationwide civil defense system—involving

federal, state, and local governments—affords an ever-increasing capability for protecting the citizen from environmental hazards and from
natural as well as man-made disasters.

During fiscal year 1971, increased emphasis was placed on finding
ways and means to increase civil defense capabilities through the dual use
of people, equipment, and dollars to meet critical peacetime community
needs. Communications, education, and training for emergencies were
stressed, and exchange of information on lifesaving emergency operations
was encouraged.

In the civil defense program, OCD works with the fifty states,
Puerto Rico, the Canal Zone, the Virgin Islands, Guam, American
Samoa, and the District of Columbia; and through the states, the office
works with more than 3,000 counties and parishes and approximately
10,000 local governments.

An objective of OCD is to provide the population of the United
States with protection from radioactive fallout that could result from
nuclear attack. In the past ten years, much progress has been made
toward this objective.

The National Fallout Shelter Survey conducted for OCD by the U.S.
Army Corps of Engineers and the Naval Facilities Engineering Command continued during fiscal year 1971 to locate potential fallout shelter
space. As in the past few years, survey operations continued to be principally of an updating nature. The operations consisted of adding new
facilities to the inventory as well as old facilities that have been improved
to meet OCD standards, and of deleting those which had been demo-
lished or would no longer qualify as shelter facilities.

By the close of fiscal year 1971, the fallout shelter inventory showed
210,382 facilities with public fallout-protected spaces for 203.5 million
people. About 132.4 million of these spaces were licensed, and 114.4
million were marked with shelter signs. There were 106,398 facilities
stocked with federal supplies sufficient to sustain 65.6 million occupants
for fourteen days, or 106.7 million occupants for eight days.

Some of the shelter space needed nationwide can be obtained by
continuing to identify fallout shelter space inherent in existing structures. There is, nevertheless, a deficit in many areas. The OCD
shelter development program has focused on architects and their con-
sulting engineers, who are encouraged to include dual-use shelter in
building designs to increase the national shelter inventory. The Office of
Civil Defense, with the assistance of universities, institutes, and professional societies, has qualified nearly 21,000 architects and engineers
in the technology of fallout shelter design and analysis. These architects
and engineers, through the application of appropriate design techniques,
are able to provide fallout protection in new buildings at little or no
additional cost. The Office of Civil Defense also offers professional

advisory services to architects and their clients through professional advisory serv'ce centers established at forty-four universities.

The Direct Mail Shelter Development System (DMSDS) administered by OCD is a program by which owners and architects of new buildings are offered technical assistance for incorporating fallout radiation protection in the design of new projects. The DMSDS uses direct-mail techniques, combined with personal contact by state or local government authorities and professional advisory service centers to assist the project designers. Contacts are made early in the design phase while there is still time to incorporate fallout protection into the building design through application of radiation protection design techniques at little or no extra cost to the owner. The use of this system has now been extended to forty-four states.

Continued as a key aspect of the civil defense program, Community Shelter Planning (CSP) and preparation of emergency operations plans develop a great amount of valuable data concerning communities. The data pertain to building types and construction, housing, traffic arteries and flow, transportation facilities and equipment, shelters and their availability to the population, locations of monitoring stations, fire and police capabilities, availability of various kinds of immediate-use resources, and many other significant items of information necessary to emergency preparedness. CSP planning is invaluable in over-all community planning to deal with environmental hazards, civil disorders, peacetime disasters, and the effects of nuclear attack. The development of emergency information materials for the public is an important part of CSP. By June 30, 1971, CSP projects completed or in process covered 2,312 counties or planning areas with a total population of 152 million people.

The improvement of the following civil defense emergency operations systems was continued to help assure effective use of shelters and conduct of recovery operations following disasters: a nationwide warning system to alert people to impending disaster; emergency communications systems to keep people informed and to enable officials to direct emergency operations; nationwide radiological monitoring and reporting systems to collect, evaluate, and disseminate information on radioactive fallout resulting from attack; and a damage assessment system to provide guidance for preattack planning and postattack operations.

Direction and control of all types of emergency actions require establishment and maintenance of a protected emergency operating center (EOC). This type of central, protected operating center—in which key officials of government can meet to co-ordinate their efforts in an emergency—is highly valuable to any community in dealing with all types of hazards. Although EOC's are promoted by OCD primarily for use in event of nuclear attack, they are frequently used by local governments during peacetime disasters. Some governors and mayors have activated their EOC's during civil disturbances. In many communities, EOC's are also in day-to-day use as the normal headquarters of government units such as civil defense and police or fire departments. Such dual use is encouraged by OCD. By the end of the fiscal year, a total of 3,784 EOC's had been established or were being established. Those centers assisted by federal funds totaled 1,096. In addition, 2,688 centers were established without federal financial assistance.

To permit broadcasting of information to the public from these EOC's, radio connections are being installed at protected commercial broadcast stations in the Emergency Broadcast System (EBS). The EBS was established to provide official information to the public in an attack emergency. As part of this system, OCD has a broadcast station protection program to provide selected stations with fallout shelter, emergency power, and the radio links to EOC's. This service enables key broadcast stations to remain on the air in a fallout environment. At the end of the fiscal year, 610 broadcast stations were included in the program.

During the year, OCD continued to provide state and local governments with financial assistance to help them obtain needed equipment and supplies for emergency purposes, as well as to help pay personnel and administrative expenses and the cost of civil defense training and emergency operating centers. By the close of the fiscal year, 4,333 political subdivisions had submitted the annual program paper required by OCD to qualify for this assistance and to obtain federal surplus property donations for civil defense use.

Public and private sector personnel—trained, educated, and experienced in emergency planning and operations—are vital to the successful development of protective measures for communities. The OCD training and Education Program supports civil defense activity nationwide at all levels of government and provides civil defense education to the public. OCD conducts civil defense training and education nationwide through the OCD Staff College, Battle Creek, Michigan; the Civil Defense University Extension Program operated by extension divisions of state universities and land-grant colleges; the Civil Defense Education Program administered for OCD by the U.S. Office of Education; the Medical Self-Help Training Program administered for the OCD by the U.S. Public Health Service; the Rural Civil Defense Education and Information Program conducted for OCD by the U.S. Department of Agriculture; and the Community Shelter Planning Training Program conducted by OCD through contract with the Graduate School of Planning, University of Tennessee.

Other programs and supporting activities continued in fiscal year

1971 included research; emergency public information; information services; liaison services with industry, labor, and organizations; and international activities.

Military support for civil defense activities received continued emphasis during the past year. All services recognize the need for a strong civil defense program and have developed comprehensive survival and recovery programs to assist civil authority in event of natural disaster or enemy attack. As a result of the publication of DOD Directive 3020.35, arrangements were made to assure reciprocity in the use of fallout shelters by the military in adjacent civilian communities and by civilians in military camps, posts, stations, and bases.

The Army has primary responsibility for providing military support. The Commanding General, U.S. Continental Army Command, and Continental U.S. Army commanders provide planning guidance to state adjutants general in the preparation of military support for civil defense plans in each of the forty-eight contiguous states. In Alaska, Hawaii, and Puerto Rico similar plans are developed by the appropriate unified command and adjutant general. Current plans call for each adjutant general, when called to federal service as a state area commander, to exercise operational control over military units made available for transattack and postattack military support missions.

At the request of OCD, the Army has recently authorized the establishment of a civil defense support detachment to augment communications and security personnel at each of the eight OCD federal regional centers located at Maynard, Massachusettes; Olney, Maryland; Thomasville, Georgia; Battle Creek, Michigan; Denton, Texas; Denver, Colorado; Santa Rosa, California; and Bothell, Washington, in the event of enemy attack or natural disaster.

III. The War in Vietnam

Operations

The redeployment of U.S. Army forces from Vietnam continued at a high rate during fiscal year 1971. Major unit strength dropped from 6 division force equivalents to 2⅔, and completion of the 150,000-man withdrawal announced by President Nixon on April 20, 1970, left Army strength in Vietnam at approximately 200,000 as the fiscal year closed.

The most significant change in operational patterns was the shift by U.S. forces from a combat role to a dynamic defense while supporting Vietnamese operations. The Vietnamese armed forces demonstrated an increasing ability to conduct large-scale and multidivisional operations. In cross-border operations in Laos and Cambodia, the South Vietnamese inflicted heavy damage upon North Vietnamese and Viet Cong forces and facilities. In line with the objectives of full South Vietnamese assumption of battlefield responsibility and American transition to advice and assistance as redeployment progresses, U.S. military field forces headquarters were redesignated regional assistance groups or commands and their activities increasingly reflected the new mission.

As U.S. combat strength decreased, a greater premium was placed on accurate and timely intelligence on the enemy. Increased knowledge of enemy movements and locations was acquired by more effective use of ground and aerial reconnaissance and closer co-ordination with intelligence agencies of the other services and the Vietnamese armed forces. Stress was placed on the interrogation of prisoners, ralliers, and other knowledgeable persons and upon exploitation of captured documents and personnel. Progressively improving information on the location, strength, and capabilities of the enemy promoted the economical and effective use of the Army's mobility and firepower. Combined American-Vietnamese intelligence operations, on which military success has depended, will provide an intelligence foundation for the Vietnamese forces as they assume full responsibility for military operations.

The April 1970 presidential announcement concerning redeployment of 150,000 U.S. troops was executed in three increments. Fifty thousand men were withdrawn by October 15, 1970, another 40,000 by December 30, and the final 60,000 by April 30, 1971. In the last month, as the first major withdrawal was being completed, the President announced a second phase under which 100,000 more men would be pulled out of Vietnam by December 1, 1971. By June 30, 1971, the terminal date of this report, redeployments that included one artillery and three infantry battalions had been applied against the new and continuing schedule. A recapitulation of strength changes due to redeployments within fiscal year 1971 indicates that U.S. forces in Vietnam were reduced from 434,000 to 254,700 by June 30, 1971. The bulk of the remaining troops were Army.

In terms of units, the 3d Brigade of the 9th Infantry Division and the 199th Light Infantry Brigade were returned to the United States, to be inactivated on October 13 and 15, 1970, respectively. By December 31, 1970, the remaining two brigades each of the 4th and 25th Infantry Divisions had been redeployed. In the increment ending April 30, 1971, the 1st and 2d Brigades of the 1st Cavalry Division (Airmobile), the 2d Brigade of the 25th Infantry Division, and the Headquarters and the 1st and 3d Squadrons of the 11th Armored Cavalry regiment were returned to the United States.

The Army continued to contribute on a major and comprehensive scale to the Vietnamization program. Army support of a combined Vietnamese Army and Regional and Popular Force numbering over 950,000 represented the leading U.S. effort under Vietnamization. One of the more important advances in the past year was the expansion of the territorial forces. Regional and Popular Force companies and platoons increased by 649, while the Vietnamese Army's artillery arm increased by about 100 two-gun 105-mm. howitzer platoons. Thirty-seven Ranger Border Defense Battalions were organized by converting Civilian Irregular Defense Groups, and the logistic and combat service support capability of the Vietnamese Army was also improved. Force structure modifications resulted in an over-all increase of about 60,000 Republic of Vietnam armed forces personnel. The U.S. sustainment promoted Vietnamese mobility, firepower, and communications for a substantive increase in combat effectiveness; U.S. equipment, training, supplies, and advice enabled the Vietnamese forces to shoulder a major share of battlefield responsibility. The magnitude of materiel support is indicated in the amounts of several types of equipment delivered to the Vietnamese armed forces to date: 855,000 small arms and crew-served weapons; 1,880 artillery pieces and tanks; 44,000 radios; and 778 helicopters and fixed-wing aircraft.

In addition to military support there were a number of Army contributions of some potential in the long-range development of the Vietnamese economy. Among them were the following activities: the Base Depot Upgrade Program with the short-term purpose of providing Vietnam with a self-sustaining rebuild capability, but with a long-range prospect of providing the country with a modest industrial base; the Line of Communication Program to improve or restore key national and inter-province roads to make a network of all-weather highways, thereby stimulating economic development through the movement of foods and goods from farms and factories to population centers; and the National Civil Telecommunications System to provide the government of Vietnam with an autonomous civil corporation to operate and maintain communication facilities to serve all military and civil clients.

Although pacification, now referred to as community defense and local development, is only one part of the total war effort in Vietnam, it is in the long run the most important part, for it is designed to produce the social, economic, and political advances that will sustain the people and their government as they seek a just peace. U.S. forces are providing material assistance, advice, and encouragement. Although progress was slow over the past year as a result of enemy reaction, economic problems, domestic strife, and cross-border military operations, advances were made in the following ways: a growing number of Vietnamese citizens enjoyed greater security than ever before; Regional and Popular Forces strength increased by more than 50,000; 96 percent of all village and hamlet and province council officials were elected; the People's Self-Defense Force improved; 30,000 enemy sympathizers rallied to the government under the Chieu Hoi program; and land distribution and reform progressed. Although internal security continued to be hampered by a shortage of competent leaders particularly at the lower echelons, the outlook for progress was good as the year closed. The community defense and local development plan, embracing self-defense, self-government, and self-development objectives, while written in the context of continued conflict with the Communists, reflects the fact that the level of this contest has changed from main force or territorial military attack to an internal security and political and economic contest. The plan serves as a basis for political and economic momentum in the event the Communist security threat further declines.

U.S. Army civil affairs agencies continued to support the operations of U.S. forces and the pacification program under the over-all direction of the Office of Civil Operations and Rural Development Support (CORDS) and in a wide range of civil affairs and civic action activities. Two civil affairs companies and four platoons operated in Vietnam during the year, chiefly at province and district levels, contributing to the over-all pacification effort by conducting water surveys, providing medical and dental care, assisting refugees, constructing schools and sanitary facilities, providing agricultural advice, and handling foreign claims. An Army engineer control and advisory detachment supported the rural development program, constructing and repairing water supply and purification systems and drilling wells. And U.S. Army military surgical teams continued to work in provincial hospitals, supporting the Ministry of Public Health by providing medical care for civilians and advice and assistance in public health and sanitation, and training Vietnamese personnel in medical care, health, and sanitation.

Logistics

Redeployment and Vietnamization were the chief concerns in the logistic field in fiscal year 1971. The withdrawal of large numbers of American soldiers and units from Vietnam meant that huge stocks of supplies and equipment had to be redistributed. Assets and requirements had to be reconciled in U.S. Army, Vietnam, and materiel excess to the needs of the Army and other U.S. agencies had to be disposed of in the most practicable and economical manner.

With the gradual disengagement from an operational logistic role in Southeast Asia, refinements could be made in transportation management. Air and surface transport were brought under tighter control to meet the needs of the user in the field more effectively. Attention centered on improving a variety of transportation programs, existing and projected, and on refining control over shipments, using airlift for selected items, and expanding the use of containerization.

Department of the Army (DA) cargo movements to and from Southeast Asia in fiscal year 1971 amounted to 36 percent of the total worldwide over-ocean movements. Passenger movements amounted to 42 percent of the total. The Military Sealift Command moved 4.6 million measurement tons of this cargo, down approximately 3 million tons from 1970. Air cargo shipments totaled 96 thousand short tons, down 45.6 thousand tons from 1970. Of the total Southeast Asia support, 71 percent of the surface cargo and 58 percent of the air cargo shipments were from the continental United States.

During fiscal year 1971, a total of 243,420 passengers were moved from the continental United States to Southeast Asia. All except 11 of these passengers traveled by air.

As the year closed, the Army was using seven ports in South Vietnam: Newport, Qui Nhon, Cam Ranh Bay, Vung Tau, Cat Lai–Nha Be, and Da Nang, all deep draft ports, and Phan Rang, a shallow draft port. Da Nang, previously a Navy port, was transferred to the Army as the year opened. Nha Trang ceased operation in August 1970 and Vung Ro terminated operations in December 1970. The average time that a ship waited for a berth in Vietnam ports declined from 20.4 days in the critical 1965 period to an average of 1.7 days in 1971. Port congestion was no longer a problem. The deep draft ports attained a daily throughput capacity of 25,755 short tons. During the first three months of fiscal year 1971, port throughput (discharge and outloading combined) in Army-operated ports in Vietnam averaged 503,-

000 short tons monthly compared with 560,000 for fiscal year 1970. This average decreased substantially in the following quarters because of a reduction in tonnage rather than in handling capacity.

The decrease in ammunition consumption in Southeast Asia, coupled with worldwide improvements in the over-all ammunition posture, led to a reduction from fifty to thirty-three in fiscal year 1971 of the number of allocable ammunition items controlled by the Department of the Army Allocation Committee, Ammunition. Insofar as Vietnam ammunition supply was concerned, two separate systems had evolved there over a period of time—one for U.S. Army forces, the other for Vietnamese forces. During fiscal year 1971 a single ammunition logistic system was begun. It calls for a merger of the U.S. and Vietnamese depot systems, with the consolidated facilities supporting all customers. Eventually, Vietnamese personnel would take over full responsibility for operating the system, with U.S. personnel as advisers. In several areas of Vietnam, the Vietnamese Army had already assumed retail support of U.S. customers as the year ended. Complete turnover will follow at a later date.

Even under the carefully phased withdrawal presently in progress, numerous actions are required from the zone of the interior out to the battlefield to insure an orderly and economical operation. Millions of dollars have been invested in the procurement, shipment, maintenance, storage, and use of U.S. materiel in Vietnam. The Army has developed a number of programs to insure the most efficient redistribution and redeployment actions. Under the Keystone program, for example, predisposition instructions were prepared to guide logistical agencies at all levels in handling the equipment that would become available as units were deactivated. Estimates were compared with continuing requirements of U.S. units remaining in the battle zone, with Vietnamization needs, with Pacific area military assistance considerations, and with Army requirements worldwide. In the fiscal year the Keystone program identified over $521.6 million in principal items for redistribution.

Another control developed by the Department of the Army was the Vietnam Asset Reconciliation Procedure, to balance major item requirements with assets in U.S. Army, Vietnam. Steps were also taken to automate the materiel management system for the Republic of Vietnam armed forces, for which the U.S. Army has been designated the primary support agency.

Equipment readiness remained high in the Pacific area in fiscal year 1971. Although large quantities of unserviceable equipment generated by the phase-down were restored in Vietnam, requirements for performing depot maintenance elsewhere increased. The Pacific depot maintenance program was funded at $43.7 million, higher than in previous years because of equipment backlog and the increased repair capability in the region. The maintenance cycle was shortened and transportation and replacement requirements reduced as a result of the Pacific regional repair capability.

Materiel and supply management attention was focused on using stocks in Southeast Asia effectively. A controlled program was instituted to carry out the transfer of major equipment items from U.S. to Vietnamese armed forces, and large quantities of consumables, secondary items, and ammunition were transferred to the Vietnamese Army. Shipments from the United States were thus limited to essential combat items, because of the major stocks already on hand in Southeast Asia.

The transfer of installations to the South Vietnamese was also accelerated, phased to the ability of the Vietnamese to maintain and operate real property. Indigenous personnel were trained to operate equipment and systems, so that during fiscal year 1971 over sixty Army installations were transferred to the Vietnamese. Such major combat bases as Engineer Hill, Camp Radcliff, Duc Pho Bronco, Phuoc Vinh–Gorvad Tay Ninh, Quan Loi, Dau Tieng, Cu Chi, and portions of Di An and Lai Khe were among those turned over.

The gradual expansion of the Vietnamese Army over the past several years and the introduction of complex equipment led to increases in support costs as well as in the costs associated with initial authorizations. Baseline equipment levels were established that enabled the Army to hold costs within departmental budget limits. Under the military assistance service-funded program for the Vietnamese Army, requirements were regularly reviewed and costs were held within program goals despite the increased scope and magnitude of combat operations.

Engineer Operations

The engineer force in Vietnam was reduced in fiscal year 1971 from about 30,000 to around 20,000 people. Engineer troop efforts during the year were distributed for the most part equally between combat and operational support and the lines of communication program. Only about 10 percent was devoted to base construction.

Engineer units continued a program of active affiliation with Vietnamese engineer units. Vietnamese land-clearing companies were trained and equipped and operated successfully in land-clearing operations in the field. Civilianization programs at various industrial sites markedly reduced troop requirements and provided valuable training and improvement in Vietnamese capabilities.

The Lines of Communication Program was the most significant construction activity in Vietnam. Initiated in 1966, it provides for a network of modern, high-speed highways connecting population centers and strategic areas in South Vietnam. The over-all objectives are to support tactical operations by providing routes for the safe movement of materiel and fire support; to accelerate the pacification program by opening up previously inaccessible areas to military forces; and to stimulate the economic development of the country by promoting the free movement of food and goods from farm and factory to market.

Under the program, 4,100 kilometers of national and interprovincial highways are being improved to provide an all-weather, two-lane, class-50 road network extending from the demilitarized zone to the Mekong Delta. By June 30, 1971, nearly 2,100 kilometers of highway had been completed by U.S. Army engineers and contract crews. The Navy completed its segment of about 400 kilometers as well. Under the Vietnamization program, Vietnamese Army units are responsible for 482 kilometers of the total.

The North Vietnamese and Viet Cong continued to use nuisance mining and booby traps against Free World forces in South Vietnam, and on an undiminished scale. Because the enemy can choose the time, place, and type of materiel to be used, this kind of action is difficult to guard against. Considerable effort was devoted in the past year to countering this kind of enemy activity through individual and unit training, surveillance and denial measures, and detection and neutralization devices. In addition to training conducted within units, a team from U.S. Army, Vietnam, visited combat units to instruct them in the latest doctrine and techniques in mine and countermine warfare. Development was begun on a data bank to assemble all aspects of mine warfare—past, present, and future—to assist the Army in meeting the problem more effectively.

Employment of unattended ground sensors and other surveillance and detection devices in areas of high enemy mining activity was used to counter specific threats. Conventional mine detectors were improved, and their issue to U.S. units was met with enthusiasm. A wide range of research projects were under way during the year to develop mine detection and neutralization hardware. The role of scatterable mines in tactical and strategic operations against enemy forces was also under continuous study.

Communications

On March 1, 1971, the 1st Signal Brigade, U.S. Army Strategic Communications Command, transferred responsibility for operation and maintenance of a major portion of the U.S. fixed communications military system in Vietnam to the Federal Electric Corporation. The change was another step in the process of reducing the U.S. military presence in Southeast Asia.

The contract is a cost-plus-award-fee type under which the Federal

Electric Corporation may receive up to a 6 percent fee for satisfactory performance or be penalized up to 2 percent for unsatisfactory performance. First year contract costs are expected to amount to about $15 million. Federal Electric Corporation was awarded the contract in competition with three other final bidders.

The contract provided initially for the operation and maintenance of thirty-eight integrated communications system (ICS) microwave and tropospheric scatter radio sites, fifteen dial telephone exchanges, and two area maintenance support facilities. The contractor was also to provide full-time maintenance support for one unmanned dial telephone exchange, one secure voice automatic switchboard, one automatic digital network switchboard for data and written messages, and maintenance support for microwave links connected to unmanned undersea cable terminals. On-call maintenance was to be provided for eight other ICS sites which would continue to be manned by U.S. Army personnel. The contractor was also required to provide communications engineering services and on-the-job training to U.S. and Vietnamese military personnel as needed to support the phase-down of U.S. forces and the turnover of communications facilities to Vietnam. The contractor provided approximately 1,600 U.S., Vietnamese, and third country civilian personnel to assume these responsibilities, releasing about 2,400 U.S. Army personnel for other duties or redeployment. The contract was written for a one-year period with renewal options and provisions for extension to other areas of Southeast Asia. Its scope will be reduced in consonance with future reductions in U.S. forces and activities. The contractor will be required to train Vietnamese personnel and be prepared to turn over a somewhat reduced system to the Republic of Vietnam as part of a single integrated telecommunications system that will serve both military and civil needs for Vietnam.

IV. Force Development

Force development in modern times is much more formal than it was in the formative period of the nation when George Washington took command of "a mixed multitude of people" and set about to develop a continental army. Today's Army operates from a series of detailed, orderly, and habitual procedures that relate to force planning and structure, organizational and operational concepts and doctrine, manpower allocation, training and schooling, and materiel requirements, among other things.

The contraction of the Army has had an understandable impact on force development. Within a period of two years the Army has been reduced by six divisions and almost 400,000 men. With $13\frac{2}{3}$ division forces in the active establishment at the close of the fiscal year, the Army was below the pre-Vietnam level of $16\frac{1}{3}$ divisions. The sharply reduced level of active forces thus placed a mounting responsibility upon the Reserve Components and a premium upon their levels of readiness. Reduction of active forces has increased the likelihood that Reserve Component units will have to be mobilized in case of emergency. Conceivably they could be called with as little as a week's notice and be deployed in an operational role sooner than they have been in the past. The Reserve Components will also have to be prepared to provide some nondivisional combat and combat support units for initial support of active Army divisions in the first sixty days of combat as a result of the loss of these types of active Army units in the current demobilization.

In addition to reductions in active Army over-all strength and units, there was a 15 percent reduction in the size of selected headquarters. On September 14, 1970, the Secretary of Defense directed the services to make such cuts against June 30, 1969, strength. In the Army the action involved headquarters with total military and civilian strengths of 27,255, requiring a reduction of 4,087 personnel in the fiscal year. In line with the need to reduce overhead costs consistent with reductions in the over-all size of the Army, the departmental headquarters programed manpower requirements in headquarters activities even below the prescribed level. The Army was able to meet and exceed the Defense Department goal with no disruption of essential mission activities.

Volunteer Army

Against the background set out in the introduction to this report, the Secretary of the Army on October 31, 1970, issued a charter to the Special Assistant for the Modern Volunteer Army (SAMVA), delineating his mission, authority, and responsibilities and designating an organization to implement them. The Modern Volunteer Army Program was designed to create conditions that would enhance the effectiveness of the Army, reduce reliance on the draft, raise the number and quality of enlistments and re-enlistments, increase service attractiveness and career motivation, and make provisions for a standby draft to meet emergencies.

In December 1970 the Chief of Staff announced a number of policy changes that represented a sharp break with tradition and demonstrated faith in the soldier's maturity and sense of responsibility. A number of time-honored practices were eliminated, including bed check and the requirement to sign in and out. Unnecessary formations were discontinued, a five-day workweek was instituted where possible, and beer was made available for sale in barracks and with the evening meal in mess halls. None of the changes interfered with training or combat missions, and none appeared to have harmed discipline; by the close of the year there were numerous indications that they had improved morale and efficiency.

Funds for the Modern Volunteer Army Program were limited in fiscal year 1971. The first priority on their use was for action to increase combat arms enlistments. As the MVA program got under way, enlistments in the infantry, armor, and artillery branches averaged about 300 a month against a requirement for 7,000. After an extensive radio and television campaign, an expansion of the recruiting force, and initiation of new and attractive enlistment options, combat arms enlistments jumped to about 4,000 per month. Although this figure is still short of the requirement, the actions appear to be working.

Congress responded favorably to the need for substantial pay increases for enlisted personnel with less than two years of service. Still needed are pay differentials for soldiers in the combat arms who qualify initially in combat arms skills and meet the high professional standards envisioned in zero draft goals.

Equally important as pay is professionalism, and experiments in improved approaches to training were conducted at four posts during the year. As some individuals learn faster than others, training is being paced at Fort Ord, California (for basic training), and Fort Benning, Georgia (for junior officers and noncommissioned officers), to the trainee's ability to meet the challenge. This approach was also instituted in unit training at Fort Carson, Colorado, and Fort Bragg, North Carolina. Although complete evaluation was not possible by year's end, early indications were sufficiently favorable to support plans to expand the procedure to all combat training centers and schools in fiscal year

1972 and throughout the Army in 1973.

Many soldiers are interrupted in their military jobs to perform kitchen police, gardening, and sanitation duties. To keep the soldier at his primary duty, civilians are to be hired to perform these housekeeping services. Subject to the availability of funds, the limited progress made in this area in fiscal year 1971 will be expanded in 1972, leading to full civilianization of housekeeping services throughout the Army by the end of fiscal year 1973.

In other moves to improve the quality of military life, barracks renovation was under way to provide more privacy and higher living standards for the soldier in troop housing. In family housing, quarters were being leased at Fort Carson on an experimental basis, and additional resources were being sought to overcome a backlog in deferred family housing maintenance. A lot of attention was centered on improving Army guest house facilities worldwide.

Food service was another area where change was taking place. Short-order mess operations were being phased in around the world, with soldier acceptance rated high. Commissaries were being improved and store hours extended. Innovations were being tested in the transportation field, including improved bus service and movement of household goods. And the Army command's Maintenance Management Inspection was eliminated and replaced with an assist-and-instruct program.

Finally, the recruiting service was expanded both in personnel and stations, and this expansion will be continued in 1972. More leased housing was provided for recruiters, and assignments and proficiency pay were stabilized. A radio and television recruiting campaign was successful, confirming the belief that paid advertising is essential to a zero draft and to the establishment of an all-volunteer Army.

Training and Schooling

Withdrawals from Vietnam and the reduction in over-all Army strength led to changes in Army manpower programs and a continued reduction in the number of new soldiers to be trained. Thus training capacity was reduced in turn; the training centers at Fort Benning, Georgia, and Fort Huachuca, Arizona, were closed, and training center operations were reduced at Fort Gordon, Georgia; Fort McClellan, Alabama; Fort Bliss, Texas; and Fort Lewis, Washington. Input to basic combat training at Fort Bragg was terminated in July 1970. Although the 410 remaining basic combat training companies operated for the rest of the year, additional reductions were in prospect for 1972.

Unit training readiness declined generally in fiscal year 1971 as a result of funding limitations, personnel turnover and shortages, and imbalances in occupational specialties. Installation support requirements were also contributing factors. Although some funds were received to ease training restrictions, they were not enough to permit division-level field training exercises for most divisions on an annual basis. Reinforcing units for Europe based in the continental United States received priority attention. As the Army adjusts to force reductions and as personnel and funding levels stabilize, unit training readiness should improve.

Exercise funds were limited in fiscal year 1971 to $15 million, the same as the authorization for fiscal year 1970 when a European reinforcing exercise (Reforger) was not held. Reforger II was conducted in the fall of 1970 at a cost of $4.9 million. The net result of the congressional action on exercise funds was to reduce by 33 percent the amount available for other fiscal year exercises.

Exercises in the United States were limited to the 82d Airborne Division and the 1st Infantry Division (Mechanized). Because of funding constraints, exercises in Europe were limited in scope, duration, and size. For a fourth consecutive year, U.S. Army, Europe, did not conduct division exercises considered essential to the proper training and combat readiness of forces. Brigade and smaller unit exercises were conducted locally and were limited in scope.

During the fiscal year the United States Army Intelligence School and Center began a move from Fort Holabird, Maryland, to Fort Huachuca, Arizona, to be completed by October 1971. The use of Fort Huachuca will permit a necessary expansion of facilities and will provide an area in which to conduct field training. Management economies will result from the concentration of activities at a single installation, the collocation of several mutually supporting activities, and the eventual closeout of Fort Holabird.

As the downward trend of Southeast Asia operations eased the demand for E–5 and E–6 noncommissioned officers and specialists, the Army turned its attention to the long-range development of noncommissioned officers. The Noncommissioned Officer Education System was established as a three-level program to formalize and upgrade the education and professional development of enlisted careerists. Basic, advanced, and senior courses were structured to enhance progressively the military education and professional development of noncommissioned officers at appropriate points in their careers. Selected basic level courses were begun during the last half of the fiscal year and full implementation of the basic and advanced levels is planned for fiscal year 1972. The senior level course is still in the planning stage.

Two new military adviser training courses were established during fiscal year 1971 at the U.S. Army Institute for Military Assistance, Fort Bragg, North Carolina: Military Assistance Security Adviser and

Military Assistance Programer Adviser. The Military Assistance Officer Command and Staff course was extended from nineteen to twenty-two weeks to provide more time for case and regional studies and individual research. This program is now limited to prospective members of the Military Assistance Officer Program.

Aviation training continued at a high level during the year. Over 4,609 active Army aviators were trained, in addition to 151 pilots from the Marine Corps, 244 from the Reserve Components, 18 from the Air Force, and 60 from foreign military units, as well as 960 from the Vietnamese Air Force.

The Army made increased use of civilian educational institutions in fiscal year 1971. Over 11,000 personnel participated in full-time schooling during the year. They studied in 160 academic disciplines at 360 colleges and universities in the United States and overseas. Over 200,000 personnel participated in off-duty study and earned over 50,000 high school diplomas, 300 undergraduate degrees, and 200 graduate degrees.

The Reserve Officers' Training Corps continued to be the largest and most economical source of second lieutenants for both the U.S. Army Reserve and the Regular Army. During fiscal year 1971, 11 new educational institutions established ROTC courses, while 5 schools discontinued their programs. The new institutions, coupled with the 15 added in fiscal year 1969, raised the number of ROTC units to 286, the highest number in the history of the program. There were 30 active applications pending at year's end from institutions desiring ROTC units.

Opening enrollments decreased 33 percent from 1970, partly because 10 institutions were converting the basic ROTC course from a required to an elective status, and because the residual impact of similar action by 39 institutions in the previous year was still being felt. Much of the decline, however, was attributable to student disenchantment with government policies, reduced draft calls, and dissident activities on campus. The frequency of dissident acts aimed at ROTC during the 1970–71 school year was about a third of that in the previous school year.

The Army awarded 819 four-year scholarships to selected high school graduates, and these plus two- and three-year types to be awarded in the summer of 1971 will keep Army scholarships at the authorized ceiling of 5,500. A legislative proposal was introduced in Congress to raise the authorized ceiling to about 10,000. A new instructional program, implemented early in the fiscal year, offers a more flexible curriculum and has helped offset much of the faculty-administration criticism that the Department of the Army was dictating what was taught in the college. Furthermore, a vigorous recruiting campaign was begun to attract more members of minority groups to the ROTC program.

Junior ROTC was conducted in 585 high schools with a total enrollment of 99,113 students. Another 28 National Defense Cadet Corps schools operated with an enrollment of 3,785. The junior program will be expanded to 650 units.

Under the Officer Candidate School program, 2,809 officers were commissioned at Fort Sill, Oklahoma, and Fort Benning, Georgia. A 14-week branch immaterial course (as opposed to the current 23-week course) was also being tested at Fort Benning. It will be evaluated in July 1972.

Missile Systems

When the President's decision to proceed with the limited deployment of a ballistic missile defense system, designated as Safeguard, was announced on March 14, 1969, three basic objectives were set forth: protection of U.S. land-based retaliatory forces against a direct attack by the Soviet Union; defense of the American people against the kind of nuclear attack which Communist China is likely to be able to mount within the decade; and protection against the possibility of accidental attacks from any source. At that time, the President also stated that "this program will be reviewed annually from the point of view of technical developments, the threat, and the diplomatic context, including any talks on arms limitations," so as to "insure that we are doing as much as necessary, but no more than required by the threat existing at that time."

The deployment requested by the President in early 1969 and approved by the Congress late that year called for the installation of Safeguard sites in two Minuteman fields—Grand Forks, North Dakota, and Malmstrom, Montana. The method of proceeding beyond this first step (Phase 1) would be dependent on future annual reviews.

The Modified Phase 2 Safeguard program for fiscal year 1971, approved by Congress in late 1970, consisted of continuing construction of the two Phase 1 sites at Grand Forks and Malmstrom and adding two additional Sprint remote launch sites at each location; deploying a third site in the Minuteman fields near Whiteman Air Force Base, Missouri; and accomplishing advanced site preparation (but not initiating construction) of a fourth site for defense of the Minuteman fields near Warren Air Force Base, Wyoming.

This year a complete and comprehensive review of Safeguard was again conducted in accordance with the President's commitment of March 14, 1969. The review reached several conclusions: that development, production, and construction progress of Safeguard had been satisfactory; that while there had been an unexplained slowdown in the deployment of current Soviet ICBM systems, tests of modifications of several missiles (SS9, SS11, SS13) continued, and even at present missile deployment levels, qualitative force improvements such as Multiple Independently Targeted Reentry Vehicles (MIRV's) could pose a threat to the survival of U.S. land-based ICBM's; that the continued deployment of Soviet Y-class submarines and the testing of a new long-range submarine-launched ballistic missile could pose a threat to the U.S. strategic bomber force; that the People's Republic of China, in an effort to develop its own ICBM system, had made progress in that direction, and that the initial system could be ready as early as 1973, with the mid-1970s a more likely time; and that although there was progress in the Strategic Arms Limitation Talks (SALT), results of the negotiations were not conclusive enough to allow a basic change of plans for Safeguard.

During this year, the research and development portion of the Safeguard program progressed satisfactorily. At Meck Island on the Kwajalein Atoll in the Pacific, the prototype missile site radar (MSR) became operational in September 1968. It met or bettered most of its design objectives, and no serious deficiencies have been found. In March 1968, checkout of the MSR data processing system was initiated, and the system was operational as a multiprocessor early in 1969. In July 1969, tracking of local targets was accomplished with the initial software, and in December 1969, two ICBM's, launched from Vandenberg Air Force Base, California, were successfully tracked.

While the MSR was being built and tested, a limited engineering development model of the perimeter acquisition radar (PAR) was constructed and activated at the General Electric Plant in Syracuse, New York, in 1969. No serious technical problems were encountered in its development. In December 1969, the Spartan interceptor successfully completed development testing at Kwajalein Island. Sprint development testing was completed in August 1970, and system tests with Sprint began soon after. As of June 30, 1971, fifteen system tests had been conducted (thirteen of these involved the firing of Sprint or Spartan missiles, and two involved only MSR tracking of an ICBM-launched test target). There were two unsuccessful tests and one partly successful test; the remaining twelve were completely successful. With the exception of an unsuccessful test on June 26, 1971, the causes of troubles were diagnosed and corrective action was taken. Study to determine the reason for the unsuccessful June 26 test was under way. There were five successful tests involving Spartan, one a salvo of two missiles guided simultaneously by the MSR and its data processor. There were also five successful tests involving Sprint, one a similar salvo launch of two Sprint missiles. Future system tests will be against more sophisticated ICBM-launched test targets as well as additional targets boosted by Polaris missiles.

The Atomic Energy Commission (AEC) has carried on its warhead testing satisfactorily. Tests of weapon features were conducted, and some weapon output measurements were made. Warhead sections with instrumented simulated warheads (no nuclear material) were flight-tested on both Sprint and Spartan missiles. Preparations were under way for further underground warhead tests and additional flight tests of certain warhead components as part of the system tests.

A summary of the year's construction status for the first two Safeguard sites at Grand Forks and Malmstrom is shown in the following table:

Sites	Components	Percent Completion June 30, 1971	Construction Completion
Grand Forks	PAR and MSR	62	December 1972
	Remote launch	6	December 1972
Malmstrom	PAR and MSR	5–10	Mid–1973
	Remote launch	No activity	Mid–1973

Design release for approximately 90 percent of all Safeguard hardware items has been made. All of the ground equipment, including the radar and associated computers and ancillary equipment for Grand Forks and Malmstrom but excluding site test and maintenance data system equipment, is being procured. Tactical software packages for Grand Forks are being manufactured. Production of the Spartan and Sprint missiles to be deployed at the first site is under way. Engineering for the Whiteman Air Force Base site is in progress. Site survey is complete for the potential Warren site.

Construction of the first Safeguard site near Grand Forks was proceeding satisfactorily. Award of the next construction contract for Malmstrom was withheld pending negotiation in accordance with Executive Order 11588 to reduce labor costs, which were in excess of government estimates. Schedules for the first site, Grand Forks, remained unaffected, but the Malmstrom schedule slipped pending award of the construction contract.

Over-all, there were no technical problems that would affect a decision to continue Safeguard deployment in fiscal year 1972.

In the year's Safeguard review, developments in the threat from other nations were carefully evaluated. The Soviets have built up their ICBM forces at a rapid rate during the past five years and, as of the end of 1970, had some 1,440 operational launchers. In April 1971, intelligence sources reported that the Soviets had started a new ICBM silo construction program. The new silos were unlike any other previously constructed, and it was not known what their purpose was or how many would be built.

The implications of these trends were still unclear. In any case, by mid-1972 the Soviets were expected to have over 1,500 operational ICBM launchers. Beyond 1972, projections concerning Soviet ICBM launchers and re-entry vehicles were less firm. Regardless of the direction in which the Soviets proceed, a key question will remain—that of the degree of missile accuracy. If the accuracy could be substantially improved, the projected Soviet SS9 missile force could pose a serious threat to the future survival of Minuteman silos.

In addition, the Soviet ICBM threat was augmented by a substantial nuclear-powered, ballistic-missile submarine fleet, which is presently a fast-growing element of the threat. At the current production rate of seven to eight such vessels per year, the Soviet Union could have by 1974 an operational force of Y-class submarines comparable in size to the current U.S. Polaris force. A longer range submarine-launched ballistic missile was also under active development, but deployment could not be estimated.

As for the strategic nuclear threat from the People's Republic of China, progress toward achieving an ICBM capability was continuing. Assessments indicated that the Chinese could attain an initial ICBM operational capability within three years after flight-testing commenced. The start of testing has not yet been confirmed, but a reduced range test of an ICBM may have occurred in late 1970. Thus, the earliest possible date for deployment would be 1973, but a year or two later is a more likely date. Significant numbers of ICBM's probably could not be deployed until late in the decade, according to the best projections.

Shortly after the United States announced in 1967 that it was to deploy the Sentinel system, the Soviets agreed to arms talks. Although progress was made in the subsequent SALT talks, the Soviet threat to the U.S. land-based strategic retaliatory forces continued to grow. Pending a formal agreement on strategic arms limitations between the United States and the Soviet Union, Safeguard proceeded on a measured program to provide for the defense of the U.S. strategic land-based system.

As the President announced two years ago, the deployment of Safeguard depended on the evolution of the Soviet and Chinese threats and on the outcome of SALT. As determined in the annual review, threat developments dictated continuation toward full Safeguard deployment pending the results of SALT.

In March 1971 the Secretary of Defense asked the Congress for authorization to implement the following proposed Safeguard program through fiscal year 1972: continue construction at Grand Forks and Malmstrom; in 1971, start construction at the Whiteman site (already authorized in the fiscal year 1971 budget); and take steps toward deployment of a fourth site at either Warren Air Force Base in Wyoming or Washington, D.C. The details of engineering, initial hardware procurement, contract bidding, and construction awards continued at Warren, along with site survey and engineering at Washington, D.C. These measures would be carried out simultaneously to provide the President maximum time to decide which location is best for deployment of a fourth site without causing unnecessary delays. Under the fiscal year 1972 request, deployment would be limited to one of the two locations.

This program would sustain progress toward U.S. strategic objectives and extend the defense of Minuteman, pending a satisfactory agreement in SALT. Additionally, the program would maintain the capability to provide for defense of the National Command Authority (NCA) as part of one option in the U.S. SALT position, and would preserve the option for deployment of area defense against small attacks at some future time. However, no funds were requested for area-only sites this year.

This program should also contribute to progress in SALT. The Soviets had indicated particular concern over a U.S. area ABM defense, but the proposed program does not request authorization for additional area defense sites beyond those which already protect Minuteman and NCA. The United States had indicated a willingness to modify its long-range plans for Safeguard if a strategically acceptable arms control agreement with the Soviet Union could be reached. By opening the option to deploy a defense of Washington, the United States is also responsive to the developments in SALT where the possibility of limiting the ABM part of an agreement to an NCA defense was discussed.

In essence, the fiscal year 1972 Safeguard program proposal continues to reflect the President's basic premise, namely, continued development at a measured, orderly, and sufficient pace, subject to review and modification as circumstances dictate.

A continuing analysis of Safeguard's capabilities indicated that while the system could cope with the threat to Minuteman for which it was designed, it would need augmentation if the threat grew beyond the ability of the presently planned Safeguard deployment. Accordingly, it was decided to initiate a program of prototype development which could augment Safeguard during the last half of this decade. This program was designated as Hardsite Defense. Rather than expanding the defense by using costly Safeguard MSR's, it would use smaller and less expensive radars to provide a cost effective augmentation to Safeguard. Budgeting for the Hardsite Defense prototype program is $65 million for fiscal year 1972.

Of the $3.7 billion authorized and approved for Safeguard through 1971, $3.3 billion had been obligated but only $2.3 billion was expended as of June 30, 1971.

Total Department of Defense acquisition costs were estimated to be $6.2 billion for the currently approved three-site program (including advanced preparation for a fourth site) and $13.7 billion for the completion of the full twelve-site Safeguard deployment, if the fastest possible schedule were to be adopted for the fiscal year 1972 budget. These estimates included an increase of $0.3 billion over last spring's $5.9 billion estimate for the currently approved three-site deployment and an increase of $3 billion over last spring's $10.7 billion estimate for the full twelve-site deployment. These increases of $0.3 billion and $3 billion resulted from a further stretch-out over last year's schedule ($0.1 billion for the three-site and $0.7 billion for the full twelve-site deployment); from added inflation factors (the inclusion of projected price level increases through deployment completion versus constant December 1969 dollar levels used for last year's estimate—$0.6 billion for the three-site and $1.9 billion for the twelve-site deployment); and from revised configuration and cost estimates (a net decrease of $0.4 billion for the three-site and net increase of $0.4 billion for the twelve-site deployment). An additional $2.5 billion in Department of Defense acquisition costs will be required after fiscal year 1971 to complete the currently approved three-site deployment and an additional $10 billion to complete the full twelve-site deployment, assuming adoption in fiscal year 1972 of an accelerated schedule.

These costs do not include an estimated $0.9 billion for nuclear warheads for the three-site or $1.2 billion for the twelve-site deployment that would be borne by the Atomic Energy Commission. The above expenditures are also exclusive of operating costs, which, for the period after completion of the deployment, are estimated to be $135 million annually for the currently approved three-site deployment and $375 million annually for the twelve-site deployment. These cost estimates, moreover, did not include certain indirect costs which were budgeted elsewhere, such as national range support, family housing, and certain Army-wide costs for hospitalization, maintenance of the Army training base, and base operations support.

Of the $1.381 billion requested in fiscal year 1972, the bulk of the funds ($1.248 billion) will be necessary for the continuation of the previously authorized sites at Grand Forks, Malmstrom, and Whiteman; $114 million is needed to carry through the work at the Warren Air Force Base site, involving advance procurement of hardware items and award of the construction contract for the major technical facilities. A lesser amount—$19 million—is required for advance preparation activities in the vicinity of Washington, D.C.

At the beginning of 1971, Congress initiated a program to provide funds for community assistance to areas affected by the impact of Safeguard installations in Montana and North Dakota. Federal departments having responsibility for administering the public laws under which communities may request funds were contacted by the Safeguard System Office, and memoranda of understanding were negotiated for processing such requests with the Departments of Transportation, Housing and Urban Development, and Agriculture and with the Public Health Service of the Department of Health, Education, and Welfare. As of June 30, 1971, a total of 70 impact assistance requests had been received for evaluation on an individual basis: 24 had been approved, 19 had been disapproved, and 27 were pending. Requests for apportionment of $7 million of the $11.8 million appropriated for such purposes were approved by the Office of Management and Budget in response to requests for assistance from affected communities in North Dakota and Montana.

Finally, during the year, congressional critics of Safeguard argued, as they had in the past, that the system would not give effective protection commensurate with its cost. In addition, critics continued to contend that deployment would have a deleterious effect on SALT. On the other hand, congressional supporters pointed to the orderly progress of the system's limited deployment, held that it added credibility to the U.S. deterrent, and saw the ABM program as leverage for use during SALT negotiations.

Various developments took place with other weapons systems during fiscal year 1971. Activations of Chaparral-Vulcan battalions continued, with six deployed in the period. SAM–D development moved ahead, nearing completion of the four-year advanced development program and ready to enter engineering development phases in the second quarter of fiscal year 1972. Deployment of the TOW antitank missile system to U.S. Army, Europe, was begun in October 1970; engineering development was completed on the Lance, and the first production contract was awarded.

Army Aviation

During the past year several aviation organizations, which had not heretofore been branch oriented, were assigned to a specific branch which assumed responsibility and became the proponent for their livelihood. Experience in Vietnam and various studies revealed that the most effective use of Army aviation results when the branch center team that is responsible for a given aircraft system actively participates in the functions that cause the "aviation" to take on the character of the branch. The armor community, for example, can look with pride upon the accomplishments of air cavalry in Vietnam.

Two rules are followed in assigning the units: aviation units are assigned to a branch based on the functions performed by the branch, for example, assault helicopter companies to the infantry since the troops which conduct combat assaults are principally infantry; and aviation units are assigned to a branch based on the primary orientation of the parent unit, for example, the artillery aviation section of an artillery group to the artillery branch. In some cases, aviation units serve a general support function which cannot be identified with a specific branch. These units continue to be the responsibility of the nonbranch aviation community at Fort Rucker, Alabama.

In the helicopter field, a program was approved in fiscal year 1971 to develop an antitank capability for the AH–1G Cobra. A limited number of Cobras will be fitted with the TOW missile to provide the earliest possible aerial antitank capability for U.S. forces in Europe. When and as the advanced attack helicopter (AAH) becomes available, the TOW-equipped Cobra will serve as a companion vehicle for less demanding tasks in units whose primary mission is reconnaissance and surveillance. The Army's future gunship force will contain the most effective possible mix of AAH's, Cobra-TOW's, and conventional Cobras.

The fourth year procurement of a five-year fixed price, multiyear contract for the OH–58A light observation helicopter was conducted during fiscal year 1971. Test and evaluation were completed early in 1971, and during the year the craft was introduced into Southeast Asia, Korea, and Europe.

The U.S. Army Board for Aircraft Accident Research found that in all major aircraft accidents where survival is possible, 44 percent of injuries and 72 percent of fatalities are caused by fires after the crash. Against this background, the Army established a twofold program: to provide a reliable fuel system, able to withstand a crash, that will reduce or eliminate the incidence of aircraft fires resulting from fuel spillage during severe but survivable crash impacts, and to improve the ballistic protection of the aircraft fuel system.

Such a system was first fielded in the new UH–1H helicopter on April 8, 1970. A refit program for older UH–1D/H craft was begun in September 1970. The system is a combination of fuel system design, impact-resistant materials, and self-sealing fuel tanks, coupled with breakaway or flexible fuel lines. The system will be installed in nearly all Army helicopters by fiscal year 1975. As of the close of the year, there had been no thermal injuries or fatalities in impact-survivable crashes involving aircraft equipped with the new fuel systems.

Ground Systems

There were several developments in ground systems during the year. The M–551 General Sheridan armored reconnaissance airborne assault vehicle, equipped with the Shillelagh missile, replaced all M–60 tanks in armored cavalry platoons in U.S. Army, Europe, thus enhancing the ability of U.S. units there to accomplish their mission. Also in Europe, U.S. Army units assigned to NATO began to receive the M16A1 rifle.

Tube artillery modernization was another area of progress. A totally new concept utilizing "soft recoil" for the 105-mm. howitzer was in advanced development, and improvements in the self-propelled 155-mm. howitzer extended its range. A new towed 155-mm. howitzer advanced into engineering development; its features included helicopter-transportable weight coupled with a significant increase in range.

Doctrine, Concepts, and Organization

In 1969 a Modern Army Selected Systems Test, Evaluation, and Review (MASSTER) activity was established at Fort Hood, Texas, to examine ways of expediting the integration of surveillance, target acquisition, and night observation equipment into the Army in the field, with emphasis on operational testing of equipment and organizations with a Southeast Asia orientation. Since that time, attention has turned to developing capabilities to meet requirements of various kinds in a variety of geographical areas, and the test role has been expanded. The Fort Hood activity now designs and conducts field tests related to doctrine, concepts, organization, and equipment—a mission especially applicable to the evaluation of the new triple capable (TRICAP) division.

The TRICAP division consists of a division base with an air cavalry combat brigade, an armored brigade, and an airmobile brigade. The division concept and the air cavalry combat brigade element will be evaluated concurrently in fiscal year 1972, with test units provided by the 1st Cavalry Division (TRICAP). The evaluations will take account of the evolution and progress in many equipment developments, ranging from an attack helicopter to automatic data processing hardware for improved command and control. Within the air cavalry combat brigade, the tank-killing helicopter will play a major role; the value of a 150-knot antitank battalion is readily apparent. Tests will develop in detail the organization and doctrine of the brigade in conjunction with the power of the companion armored brigade and the mobility of the associated airmobile infantry brigade. The results will be applied in the development of the entire TRICAP division.

In June 1970 the Army began a program to improve command and control capabilities through an integrated battlefield control system. The objective was to provide a fully integrated tactical command and control system, matched to similar systems in the other services, to be used by the Army in the field in the post-1976 period. Concurrent with this development, the Army reviewed the management of its development of tactical automatic data processing systems. In recognition of the need for systems relationship, commonality, compatability, and interoperability, not only between Army systems but between Army and other service tactical data systems, a single project manager for Army Tactical Data Systems was designated, thus centralizing at Fort Monmouth, New Jersey, the responsibility in this field and collocating it with the Army's tactical communications system developments there. The project manager will be responsible initially for the Army's Tactical Fire Direction System, Air Defense Control and Coordination System, and Tactical Operational System.

The process of matching unit organization, staffing, and equipment to unit mission is a never-ending one. As missions change, increasing in scope, size, and complexity, new and more sophisticated equipment comes into play, and personnel changes are required. Equipment requirements must be constantly reviewed and authorization documents regularly validated to insure that military units with unique and special missions have the best possible balance in personnel and equipment to carry out their missions. This is the purpose of the Equipment Survey Program.

The Army Authorization Documents System (TAADS) is a primary source of information for planning budgets, procuring equipment, and determining personnel requirements. Minor inaccuracies in unit documents become major problems at Department of the Army headquarters where all unit requirements are consolidated in TAADS. The purpose of the Equipment Survey Program is to insure that the TAADS data base reflects equipment actually required by units, and that outdated equipment is removed from authorization and issue lists.

Surveys were conducted during the fiscal year in twenty-seven units, resulting in a total of $61 million in equipment changes: $18 million in additions and $43 million in deletions, a net reduction of $25 million in equipment authorizations. The trend is expected to continue as approximately 2,000 units are surveyed.

Chemical Warfare and Biological Research

Following President Nixon's ban, announced in fiscal year 1970, of all types of biological warfare, the Army prepared plans for disposing of stocks stored at various locations. Public Law 91–190, the National Environmental Policy Act of 1969, required the preparation of an environmental impact statement covering disposal operations, and its review by federal, state, and local authorities. Both the disposal plan and the environmental impact statement were reviewed by the Army Staff, the Office of the Secretary of Defense, and the Department of Health,

Education, and Welfare. After subsequent approval by the Council on Environmental Quality, the environmental impact statement was reviewed by the Departments of Agriculture and Interior, the Environmental Protection Agency, and each state where disposal would be conducted. Disposal would involve antipersonnel material at Pine Bluff Arsenal in Arkansas, and anticrop material at Rocky Mountain Arsenal in Colorado, Beale Air Force Base in California, and Fort Detrick in Maryland.

Disposal of antipersonnel agents and weapons was begun on May 17, 1971. Disposal of anticrop material was delayed by the review process, but would probably begin in the summer of 1971, extending over the course of a full year at Rocky Mountain Arsenal, six months at Fort Detrick, and three months at Beale Air Force Base.

Meanwhile, the disposal at sea of obsolete chemical munitions was completed in August 1970 without incident. Stocks of munitions encased in concrete vaults were shipped by rail from Anniston Army Depot, Alabama, and Blue Grass Army Depot, Kentucky, to Sunny Point Ocean Terminal, North Carolina. There they were loaded on a vessel hulk, towed to sea, and sunk in more than 16,000 feet of water. Operation Chase, as it was called, went smoothly, with no transportation or ecological problems, as had been feared by many citizens. More than 3,000 letters of protest or inquiry were received by government officials and answered by the Department of the Army. As an alternative to sea dump for disposal of obsolete and unserviceable chemical munitions, the Army has developed comprehensive plans and technology for safe disposal of this material on land—plans which will have inconsequential or no impact on the environment.

V. Personnel

In terms of national defense, personnel consists of the individuals —military or civilian—required to carry out the mission assigned to the armed forces, and of the full range of administrative functions relating to the recruitment, assignment, discipline, housing, subsistence, pay, health, advancement, protection, and retirement of the Army's manpower.

Military Personnel

During fiscal year 1971, Army strength decreased from 1,324,000 to 1,123,810. Included in the total were 148,950 officers, 971,872 enlisted personnel, and 2,988 cadets. There were 22,969 officers acquired during the year. A total of 156,075 men were inducted into the Army and 157,627 men and women were acquired by first enlistments, representing a decrease of 42,617 inductions and 19,630 enlistments from fiscal year 1970.

Officer procurement was reduced by one-third to meet lower year-end manpower authorizations. This reduction was accomplished by limiting direct appointments and reducing accessions from Officer Candidate School (OCS) and Reserve Officers' Training Corps (ROTC) programs. OCS was reduced from 6,500 to 2,809 by soliciting the voluntary withdrawal of approved applicants and candidates, while the number of ROTC graduates scheduled for active duty was reduced from 15,500 to 9,237 through an active-duty and active-duty-for-training adjustment under which a random selection of officers was made to meet Army requirements. Maximum use was made of volunteers, and graduates not selected for active duty were placed on active duty for training for three months or for the length of their basic branch course, whichever was longer.

It is Army policy that permanent-change-of-station travel for military personnel is based upon necessity. Excessive movement of personnel is expensive, disruptive to readiness, and detrimental to morale. Efforts are being made to reduce both the number and frequency of moves in order to achieve greater continuity, assignment stability, and monetary savings. Permanent changes of station were reduced to the minimum, consistent with short tour requirements and equity in the sharing of hardship duties. The redeployment from Southeast Asia had the greatest impact on personnel stability.

As the year closed, short tour requirements had decreased and normal rotation policies were being restored. With Army strength down 15 percent from fiscal year 1970 and requirements in Vietnam easing, total permanent changes of station were down 21 percent, and costs for such travel were down 7 percent.

As the Army moves toward an all-volunteer force, an effective and fully manned recruiting service is essential to success. Reduced reliance on the draft requires aggressive, imaginative, and productive programs to attract an increasing number of volunteers to replace not only draftees but a large number of draft-induced volunteers. The efforts of the U.S. Army Recruiting Command will be important. Thus the Army during the year proposed that the size of the recruiting force be more than doubled, from 2,969 to 6,080 by the end of the coming fiscal year.

New mental standards under which the Army accepts men from among those disqualified for service before October 1, 1966, were continued under the over-all enlisted procurement program. The mandatory quota was revised for fiscal year 1971 from 12 to 8 percent of total new enlistees, a change necessitated by the decreasing size of the Army and of low-skill jobs available for men with lower mental abilities. The long-range objective is to eliminate quota controls for this program as draft calls approach zero.

A college graduate utilization program was continued to insure that the 25,296 degree-holders who entered during fiscal year 1971 were given challenging and demanding assignments. At the same time, the program to make the greatest possible use in military jobs of skills acquired in civilian life was emphasized, and over 24,000 inductees were assigned duties based on skills acquired in private life, thereby promoting job satisfaction and increased motivation while reducing training costs. The Selective Service System at the Army's request assisted in the search for specially qualified personnel by incorporating a request for such information in induction notices. Reception stations also tested personnel in thirty-five military occupational specialty (MOS) areas to identify candidates for the direct award of an MOS.

Under the Army's community service program, attention was focused on personal problems encountered by junior grade personnel and their families. At the modern volunteer Army test sites, attention was centered on improving the ways in which new families are oriented to Army life; on developing more effective techniques for assisting them during relocation and emergencies; and on helping them to meet financial problems. Model programs in these areas were developed and tested for adaptation at other installations during the coming year.

In addition to programs related to individuals entering the service, the Army continued a number of programs to help those who were leaving. Project Transition, funded at $8.9 million and with 391 vocational guidance counselors, was extended to Alaska and Hawaii in addition to major installations in the continental United States, where, as the year closed, its services were available at fifty-six installations. Resources were being reprogramed to offer preseparation vocational counseling and job placement services overseas. The Army also supported Department of Defense actions to match Project Transition and Project Referral operations with the Jobs for Veterans Program; the Army Command Information Program was used to inform servicemen, while Army National Guard and Reserve participation was sought in extending the Jobs for Veterans Program to the local community level.

The Department of the Army, as executive agent for the Department of Defense, conducted an unusual civilian police recruiting program for the District of Columbia's Metropolitan Police Department during the fiscal year. Attention was centered on personnel leaving the various services. The program offered these people an early release of up to 150 days as an inducement to join the police department; sixty-two men joined the civil force in the nation's capital.

A number of actions were taken during the year to improve the Army's correctional program. Because of the importance of cadre support, commanders of Army confinement facilities were directed to establish and conduct on a continuing basis an in-service training program in the care, custody, and correction of prisoners. Eighteen-month stabilized tours at confinement facilities were established for the commanding officer, provost sergeant, and correctional supervisor and for correctional treatment and prisoner service chiefs. The Military Police table of organization was amended to provide for an Army psychologist or social work officer for each 250 prisoners confined at Army stockades to direct prisoner counseling. In stockades with less than 250 prisoners, a social work and psychology specialist for each 50 prisoners is authorized for prisoner counseling, with technical supervision provided by a social work or psychology officer from the local medical facility. Qualified cadre support was further enhanced by a policy change which requires that personnel assigned at stockades to duties as prisoner work supervisors be correctional specialists; the practice of using guards detailed from other units was prohibited.

The correctional training program at the U.S. Army correctional training facility was expanded to include refresher training in military subjects for prisoners who have completed basic combat training or possess a military occupational specialty and are returning to duty status. At the U.S. Disciplinary Barracks, a prototype work-release program was developed with a view to aiding prisoners during the transition period of release from confinement and return to military or civil life as useful citizens. The work-release program will be implemented during the first quarter of fiscal year 1972. In addition to temporary home paroles authorized in emergency situations, a program was adopted which authorizes commandants of disciplinary barracks to grant special temporary home paroles to selected prisoners during religious holiday periods. The purpose of the temporary home parole program is to strengthen family relationships, provide an incentive and reinforcement for positive behavior and morale, and provide an indication of future prisoner adjustment if released on regular parole or restored to duty.

Plans and designs for new confinement facilities based on modern correctional principles were developed, and construction was begun at critical locations; a priority list of stockades to be modernized during fiscal years 1973–77 was also established. A policy to improve prisoner services was adopted, which requires commanding officers of installation confinement facilities to develop appropriate educational courses for prisoners as part of the correctional treatment program. Branch field libraries are to be established, equipped with enough materials to support the prisoner capacity of the facility.

Because of the sensitive nature and problems of prisoners in administrative and disciplinary segregation, they require judicious supervision. Confinement facilities were required to have mature noncommissioned officers, experienced in correctional supervision, in charge of administrative and disciplinary segregation cell sections at all times. Provisions were also made for daily visits by chaplains and counselors. Authority of confinement facility commanders to impose restricted diet as punishment for prisoners in disciplinary segregation was abolished, although commanders were authorized to prescribe a reduced diet in accord with sedentary conditions. Daily rations of prisoners in disciplinary segregation are not to be less than 2,100 calories, and daily exercise is not to be less than an hour. In connection with prisoner employment, armed guards were prohibited on outside work details, and unsentenced prisoners were permitted to waive their right to work and be billeted separately from sentenced prisoners.

The Army Safety Program also received some attention during the past year. Each year since 1966 the National Safety Council has selected an organization with an outstanding record in accident prevention to present formally before the council the policy, philosophy, and characteristics of its accident prevention program. In 1970 the Department of the Army was the featured agency. The presentation was made at Chicago, Illinois, on October 28, 1970, in ceremonies at which the council presented to the Army its Safety Award of Honor for accident prevention.

The Army participated in several programs of broad domestic and nonmilitary character during the past year. One was the so-called Sky Marshal Program. When, on September 11, 1970, the President responded to a rash of political hijackings of U.S. commercial aircraft by ordering that armed guards be placed aboard appropriate flights to protect the passengers, the Department of Defense was designated to provide 800 military men on detail to the Department of Transportation to serve as sky marshals. The military part of the program was conducted by the Department of the Army, to assist the Department of Transportation in screening, training, deploying, and supervising military personnel from all the services who participated voluntarily as federal air security specialists to combat air piracy. As the executive agent, the Army formed a task group under the direction of the Provost Marshal General. The Army provided selected equipment, a training site at Fort Dix, New Jersey, and training support. During the period from October 5, 1970, to May 17, 1971, 845 enlisted volunteers from all the services served as sky marshals and another 50 performed liaison duties. The Department of Defense paid the initial military costs and normal military pay and allowances for what was called Operation Grid Square (estimated at $4.5 million), to be reimbursed by the Department of Transportation when funds are appropriated by Congress. As follow-up support, the Department of the Army provided facilities at Fort Belvoir, Virginia, as a training site for the Department of the Treasury's Civilian Sky Marshal Program. Training here was conducted from December 28, 1970, to May 21, 1971, and in the latter part of the fiscal year the graduates of the Treasury school replaced the military sky marshals.

Both the active Army and the Army Reserve Components have actively supported the domestic action program. The Army is well equipped to join with other public and community organizations in the national effort to overcome the nation's domestic problems. Among the domestic actions in which the Army has participated are the following activities: summer and student employment of disadvantaged youths; visits to Army installations and overnight encampments; community projects such as ecology and athletic programs; loans to other federal agencies to support youth activities; equipment loans to assist disadvantaged citizens in emergencies; and unit projects undertaken in conjunction with training exercises. During fiscal year 1971, 700,000 disadvantaged youths were provided one and one half million man-weeks of educational, recreational, and cultural opportunities at Army installations, and 16,-313 youths were given meaningful work experience training through the Army's summer and student employment programs for disadvantaged youths.

Health and Medical Care

The rate of admissions to hospitals and quarters for Army active duty personnel worldwide during fiscal year 1971 was 338 per 1,000 average strength per year, 8 per 1,000 less than the 346 reported for fiscal year 1970. The noneffective rate, representing the average daily number of Army active duty personnel in an excused-from-duty status due to medical causes per 1,000 average strength, was 16.9 as compared with 17.6 in the previous year. Noneffectiveness due to wounds incurred in action (WIA) declined to 3 per 1,000 from 4.2 in fiscal year 1970.

The following table shows the rates at which men were admitted to hospitals and quarters in Vietnam and other areas for diseases and injuries as well as for all causes, along with the incidence rates of malaria and certain other conditions which tend to cause a high proportion of noneffectiveness in one or more of the areas.

ADMISSIONS TO HOSPITALS AND QUARTERS AND INCIDENCE OF
SELECTED CONDITIONS—U.S. ARMY PERSONNEL ON ACTIVE DUTY
FISCAL YEAR 1971

(Rates per 1,000 average strength per year)

	World-wide	CONUS Army Areas	Oversea Areas Total	Europe	Pacific	
					All Areas	Vietnam
Admissions						
All causes	338	353	323	199	392	434
Disease	290	323	262	170	313	340
Nonbattle injury	39	30	43	29	50	56
Wounded in action	9	....	18	...	29	38
Incidence						
Malaria	8.01	4.24	11.95	0.49	19.24	24.36
Diarrheal diseases	21.08	16.18	27.84	12.78	35.44	40.73
Acute upper respiratory infection and influenza	93.72	139.46	41.11	33.04	43.09	45.42
Skin diseases, including dermatophytosis	12.28	5.76	18.93	1.90	29.50	36.52
Neuropsychiatric conditions	16.16	13.80	18.48	9.35	23.94	25.17
Hepatitis viral	4.49	3.98	5.03	0.50	7.85	8.19

In the five-year period from June 1966 to June 1971, over 1 million units of whole blood were shipped from continental U.S. donor centers under the Military Blood Program. Over 50 percent of the total came from Army donor centers. The Military Blood Program Agency of the Office of The Surgeon General of the Army is staffed by medical officers from all the services. Military Blood Program support in Southeast Asia is a major factor in the reduced death rate of hospitalized wounded personnel. At no time has there been an over-all shortage of whole blood in Vietnam.

The most acute shortage of medical officers in the Army is in the general duty area. Medical generalists have traditionally provided medical service in maneuver battalions and troop clinics. To ease the shortage in general duty medical officers—those with the military occupational specialty of 3100—a physician's assistant program was established under which fully trained back-up personnel would provide medical services of certain kinds formerly reserved for doctors. In March 1971 the Department of Defense answered a number of questions concerning the nature of the position and the training and degree of independence of the physician's assistant by issuing the following definition:

The military Physician's Assistant is a skilled health professional who is not a physician but who by experience and formal training has become qualified to perform certain tasks formerly undertaken only by a physician. He works under the supervision of a medical officer, though he may at times serve some distance from the physician and receive instruction and guidance by telephone or other means of communication. He may perform selected tasks delegated to him by the physician supervisor who is responsible for his actions. His principal duties will involve direct contact with patients to obtain medical histories and to perform physical examinations, order appropriate laboratory and x-ray studies, interpret and record these data and prescribe limited therapy. He is considered to meet the criteria of the "Type-A" Physician's Assistant as defined by the Board of Medicine of the National Academy of Science, May 1970.

The Army Medical Department program proposes to alleviate the shortage of Army physicians and meet field medical requirements by using physicians' assistants. In the clinical environment the assistants would fill the gap between the patients and the highly skilled medical specialists who form the larger proportion of Army physicians. Assistants would extend the capabilities of the physician by relieving him of the burdens of routine examinations, tests, and administration, which do not require his level of expertise. The physician would be able to spend more time on duties which only he can perform.

The program would provide eighteen months of additional training to selected, highly qualified active Army enlisted medical specialists. Individuals selected for the physician's assistant program would have a minimum of three years of patient treatment experience and would probably have completed a forty-week training course prior to selection. After rigid screening, candidates would receive twelve months of didactic training and reinforcing clinical practice, followed by a supervised six-month applicatory assignment in an Army hospital. Candidates would then return to school for final examinations, and upon successful completion of all course requirements, would be granted a warrant in the Army of the United States.

Some form of an armed forces health professions scholarship program has been before the Congress for more than twenty years, but despite continuing interest, no serious move has been made to enact legislation. Today, with increased interest in the need to obtain additional physicians, dentists, and other health specialists under volunteer Army–zero draft conditions, two measures have been placed before Congress to relieve a fast-developing medical personnel crisis. One proposal would permit participants to pursue up to four years of graduate study in a health profession while on active duty as commissioned officers. They would receive full pay and allowances, and all tuition and other educational expenses would be paid. In return, they would incur an active-duty obligation of not less than one year for each year spent in the program. About 825 officers a year would participate in the program leading to a maximum authorization of 2,500. In the other program, similar in many respects, the participants would be Reserve Component officers not on active duty. Either program would appear to be essential in the light of the fact that present medical officer procurement programs are supported by conscription. With plans to eliminate the draft by the end of fiscal year 1973, lead time will rapidly disappear. The situation is further intensified by the poor prospects for passage of a medical school bill which would provide relief on a long-term basis.

Housing

Based on long-range strength and deployment estimates the Army needs a total of 353,440 housing units for eligible families. Available family housing on and off post totals 220,600 units. This figure includes about 130,000 adequate military-owned or -controlled units that are operated and maintained by the Army. After taking into consideration the limitations imposed by the Department of Defense on construction of new family housing, there is a remaining deficit of 62,800 units. A total of 1,700 units was authorized for the Army in the fiscal year 1971 program, and Congress is considering approval of 1,920 units for the 1972 program. The provision of adequate housing for all married personnel is recognized as an ultimate goal in the development of the all-volunteer Army, which would about double the deficit to 135,000 units. Initial steps to achieve this goal will be incorporated in the Army's five-year financial proposal beginning in fiscal year 1973.

There is also a substantial deficit in bachelor housing for officers and enlisted men. Army personnel are still housed in obsolete World War II buildings at many locations. About 4,000 new bachelor officer quarters spaces and 110,000 enlisted men's barracks spaces are needed. To overcome the backlog, annual outlays of $63 million for barracks and $6 million for bachelor officer quarters would be required over the next ten years.

Legal Affairs

A December 1969 amendment to the Economic Opportunity Act of 1964 authorized members of the armed forces and their immediate families to obtain legal services from the Office of Economic Opportunity in cases of extreme hardship, provided such services were funded by the Department of Defense. With the approval and support of the American Bar Association, the Secretary of Defense on October 26, 1970, directed the establishment of a pilot program to ascertain whether these services could be better provided by military attorneys through the expansion of traditional military legal assistance programs. The new program would support only those soldiers and their dependents who cannot afford legal fees without undue hardship, and who therefore would probably not seek assistance from civilian sources. Under this standard, practically all members in the grade of E–4 and below and their dependents would be eligible for the program.

The Army was the first military department to obtain authorization from one of the states, New Jersey, for a fully operational test. In early November 1970, appropriate officials of the Monmouth County Bar and Burlington County Bar Associations considered the matter and gave their support. The Board of Trustees of the New Jersey State Bar Association raised no objections, and on January 4, 1971, the Army was advised that the Supreme Court of the State of New Jersey had approved the project.

Following a series of meetings with representatives of various groups associated with the practice of law in New Jersey, the test began at Forts Monmouth and Dix. Experience in New Jersey from February 1 through June 30, 1971, indicates that cases fall into four general categories: small claims, landlord and tenant, domestic relations, and criminal offenses. Statistics indicate that only 3 percent of all prospective clients interviewed had legal problems acceptable under the program. No matters were handled in which the client could afford the services of a civilian attorney. Many disputes were settled out of court; most of the comparatively few cases that reached litigation were resolved in favor of the serviceman client. In criminal cases, initially offenders were represented by military attorneys only for nonindictable types of criminal offenses. More recently, however, the Public Defender of New Jersey requested that military attorneys also represent indigent servicemen accused of felonies.

The New Jersey Bar has collectively and individually encouraged this program. It has provided Judge Advocate General's Corps officers with workshops and materials, which have greatly helped military lawyers in trying cases before the New Jersey courts. The American Bar Association Standing Committee on Legal Assistance for Servicemen held its spring 1971 meeting at Fort Monmouth to examine the New Jersey program. The committee's report enthusiastically encouraged the adoption of this concept in other states. The Army is endeavoring to establish similar programs in Kansas and Colorado and, jointly with the Air Force, in Alaska.

The Department of the Army is encouraged by the initial success of the experiment. Military clients of limited means now have access to first-class legal services, thereby enhancing morale; the Army's reputation for taking care of its own is improved, a favorable consideration in volunteer Army terms; the civilian bar is supported in the dispensing of justice; and the goals of the legal profession are advanced.

For several years the Army and the Internal Revenue Service have jointly conducted an Overseas Income Tax School Program. This project, supported by the other services, trains Department of Defense civilian and military personnel as income tax assistants for their respective offices and units. During January and February 1971, thirteen schools were conducted in nine countries with 849 students in attendance, including 530 officers, 263 enlisted men, and 56 civilians. In addition to providing knowledgeable advisers to assist servicemen in filing their federal and state returns, the program promotes good citizenship.

During fiscal year 1971, Army claims obligations as monitored worldwide by the U.S. Army Claims Service amounted to $28.5 million in settlement of 96,783 claims against the U.S. government. Recoveries from carriers, warehousemen, insurers, and other third parties amounted to $2.1 million.

Civilian Personnel

During the year the Army's almost half-million civilians worked in an atmosphere of declining forces and missions and of increasing emphasis on civilian support to a modern volunteer army.

Civilian personnel strength declined by 5.2 percent in fiscal year 1971, from 513,000 on June 30, 1970, to 486,000 on June 30, 1971. Civilian strength in the United States declined 3.8 percent. The percentage decrease in numbers of foreign national employees was over twice that of U.S. citizens; their number dropped from 135,200 to 121,800, a decline of 9.9 percent. Major reductions occurred in Vietnam, Korea, Thailand, Japan, and Italy.

Concerted effort was made by all commands to accomplish these reductions through attrition and restriction on recruitment. Where these methods were not feasible, some employees were separated by reduction-in-force procedures. High priority was given to placing these employees with other federal agencies or private employers. Department of the Army and Department of Defense placement programs were effective in locating employment opportunities for many employees who did not restrict their geographic availability.

The department's Equal Employment Opportunity Program proved again to be innovative, due to the formulation of numerical goals and timetables, which were Army-wide in scope, in the Equal Employment Opportunity Plan of Action. Some of these goals were proposed by the Secretary of the Army in a speech before the Equal Employment Opportunity Command Institute last year. After final approval in August 1970, the plan was sent to the field with instructions to establish numerical goals at the installation level as well. This concept of goals and timetables has been endorsed by the United States Civil Service Commission, and all federal agencies will be permitted to use them in resolving equal employment opportunity problems.

The first annual Secretary of the Army awards for honorary recognition for outstanding achievement in equal employment opportunity were presented to two members of the U.S. Army Materiel Command. Commemorative plaques and citations were presented to Colonel Luther G. Jones, Jr., commanding officer of the Army Aeronautical Depot Maintenance Center at Corpus Christi, Texas, and to Robert A. Cole, Sr., equal employment opportunity officer of the Army Mobility Equipment Command in St. Louis, Missouri. Colonel Jones's significant achievements in his management of the Army's huge helicopter overhaul and repair center include establishment of an annual seminar entitled "Operational Understanding," which brings together community leaders, educators, and business and professional associations to discuss problems in equal employment opportunity; and a continuing program in support of equal opportunity for women in employment, training, promotion, and assignment. Mr. Cole became equal employment opportunity officer at the Army Mobility Equipment Command in October 1967, and within three years the command exceeded the goal of achieving the same minority group representation in the work force as in the population of the St. Louis metropolitan area.

A wide variety of special employment programs were emphasized again this year. Programs such as the President's Stay-in-School Campaign, Summer Employment for Youth, Project Hire, Veterans' Readjustment Appointment Program, and others became more important this year due to decreasing employment opportunity in private industry. Reduced funding at Army installations somewhat restricted the scope of these programs, but despite funding problems, the special employment programs were successful. Approximately 670 Veterans' Readjustment Appointments were made in fiscal year 1971, about 1,500 students were hired under the Stay-in-School Campaign, over 16,000 young people were hired in the Summer Employment for Youth Program, and about

180 trainees were hired under Project Hire (a combination hiring and training program for Alaskan natives).

Significant advancements were made toward the development of a comprehensive automated information system for civilian personnel. A limited system was planned and developed to provide primarily for the automation of quarterly minority employment statistics commencing January 1, 1971. A controlled expansion of the established system is planned. It will be undertaken based on experience gained from the current operation, on the determination of additional information requirements warranting automation, on cost effectiveness, and on the use to which an expanded system can be put by all levels of command within the Army structure.

Labor relations continued to require a great deal of attention from the department this year as the expansion of labor unions continued. The number of Army employees covered by exclusive recognition on June 30, 1971, totaled 203,800, an increase of 39,000 over the previous year's total. The number of exclusive bargaining units increased from 515 to 661 in the same period. Increased organizing efforts by unions seeking to convert formal units to exclusive recognition by July 1, in order to retain dues-withholding arrangements, and the inclusion of National Guard and nonappropriated fund employees in the federal labor relations statistics contributed to this growth of unionism.

During the past year, continued emphasis was placed on implementing the provisions of Executive Order 11491 on labor relations and regulations issued by central labor-management relations authorities. There was increased activity by the Assistant Secretary of Labor for Labor-Management Relations as landmark decisions were made on bargaining unit determinations and unfair labor practice cases. The Federal Labor Relations Council and the Federal Service Impasses Panel also became viable instruments in the third-party review process. Department of the Army guidance was developed and issued to supplement significant decisions made by these authorities.

A strike contingency plan was published in order to prepare Army managers to deal with possible work stoppages by Army employees. A guide for dealing with such stoppages was developed and distributed to major commands to assist in the preparation of their individual contingency plans.

Eight regional seminars on labor-management relations were conducted during June 1971. These seminars were designed to acquaint installation commanders and managers with experience and new developments in the labor-relations field since the original orientations on Executive Order 11491 were conducted in January 1970. Over five hundred military and civilian executives attended these follow-up seminars.

Based upon the Secretary of the Army's decision that military activities in the Panama Canal Zone were not covered by the provisions of the executive order, a comprehensive labor-management relations policy statement was developed which continued the policy of granting only formal recognition to labor organizations in the Canal Zone. This policy shaped the labor-management relationships of all U.S. military activities in the Canal Zone.

Civilian career programs provide for the orderly intake, training, placement, and career progression of civilian employees in most professional and technical occupations. These programs, which have been steadily expanded during the last twelve years, now cover fifteen career areas and almost 85,000 Classification Act employees.

The new Transportation Management Career Program established this year is the most recent addition to the list. Two other Army-wide programs for communications management and manpower management are currently being developed.

During the year the Army was designated by the Deputy Secretary of Defense to be executive agency for the development and implementation of a DOD-wide Career Program for Comptroller-Financial Management. The Department of the Army was given wide latitude to draw upon the other services as needed in the development of the DOD program. A working group was formed with representatives from the U.S. Air Force and Navy, and a draft DOD directive on the program was near completion as the year closed.

The suggestion program continued to be an important factor in increasing the efficiency and reducing the cost of operating the department. During fiscal year 1971, civilian employees submitted 68,573 suggestions, 19,536 of which were adopted, resulting in first-year tangible benefits of $58,597,111. Military personnel submitted 50,516 suggestions; 3,643 of these were adopted resulting in first-year measurable benefits of $13,095,544. This figure is somewhat lower than last year because of the turbulence created by reorganizations and reductions in force.

Two top suggesters were selected as Army Economy Champions for fiscal year 1970 and were given medals and cash awards. Captain Jackson L. Schultz, U.S. Navy, Deputy Commander, Military Ocean Terminal, Oakland Army Base, and Lionel P. Hernholm, Equipment Analyst, U.S. Army Combat Developments Command, were the winners, each with a suggestion that resulted in over $1.7 million in measurable first-year benefits.

Army civilians were also given prominent recognition outside the Army during the year. Dr. Fred Leonard, scientific director of the Army Biomechanical Research Laboratory, Walter Reed Army Medical Center, was one of five individuals to receive the President's Award for Distinguished Federal Civilian Service, the highest honor for federal career employees. Dr. Leonard, a world-renowned medical research scientist, was honored for his pioneering efforts in the development of advanced surgical repair materials and other techniques and devices which have saved critically wounded soldiers.

Charles F. Mullaly, Director of Civilian Personnel for the Department of the Army, was this year's recipient of the Society for Personnel Administration's Stockberger Award, given annually to a person in public or private life who has made an outstanding contribution toward improvement of personnel management at any level of government. Mr. Mullaly's leadership enhanced the image of the Army as an employer and influenced the shape of personnel management programs throughout the federal community.

Conversion of Army blue-collar employees to the new Coordinated Federal Wage System was completed except for employees who are paid on Lithographic and Printing, Hydroelectric Power Plant Operating, Marine and Floating Plant, and other special wage schedules. The Civil Service Commission regulation on environmental differentials paid for exposure to various degrees of hazards, physical hardships, and working conditions of an unusual nature became effective November 1, 1970, resulting in pay increases for a large number of Army employees. Department of the Army representatives continue to participate actively on wage committees of the Civil Service Commission and the Department of Defense in the development of regulatory material related to the Coordinated Federal Wage System.

There is a growing recognition that the Army service school system does not adequately train Army officers to supervise civilian personnel. During fiscal year 1970 a significant remedial step was taken in response to an invitation from the commandant of the Army Management School. A substantial block of subject matter in civilian personnel administration was made an integral part of a CONARC-directed common elective package of instruction entitled "Installation Management." In addition, the Deputy Chief of Staff for Personnel co-operated with the U.S. Army War College faculty in developing a personnel management elective at the college for academic year 1971, and a session entitled "Civilian Personnel System" was developed for use at the U.S. Army Command and General Staff College.

The modern volunteer army concept and the test project placed new emphasis on the role of the civilian in support of the soldier. Professionalizing the duties of the soldier and relieving him of quasi-military duties will probably result in a higher ratio of civilians to soldiers in the department.

VI. Social Concerns

Since the Army is a reflection of the society from which it springs, the citizens entering military service naturally bring with them the variety of attitudes and practices, both desirable and objectionable, that shape the national environment. Army problems today differ from those of the past, more in degree than in nature. Military services have always had to cope with abuses and, by regulation and leadership, limit their effects in the never-ending task of building and maintaining efficient and effective forces.

Drug Abuse

In the closing month of the year, the President of the United States directed that the critical national problem of drug abuse be given priority attention in the country and in the armed forces. The Army began a series of actions founded on nonpunitive and compassionate considerations, reflecting a national trend to this kind of philosophy. As a first step, a program was instituted in Vietnam to identify drug users before they left for home, to refer them for immediate detoxification (physical withdrawal) in Vietnam, and to provide followup treatment in the United States. Identification, if not voluntary on the part of the individual, is made through biochemical tests of urine, confirmed by separate chemical analysis. Where the use of drugs is confirmed, individuals are referred to a quarantine area for medical observation and detoxification. After two to seven days of treatment, depending on the degree of drug dependency, the individual is sent to a hospital in the United States for further short-termed rehabilitative treatment.

Those whose terms of service are expiring and who need and desire treatment for drug dependency are given an opportunity for at least thirty days of treatment in military facilities if the Veterans Administration or civilian treatment programs are not capable of providing care at the time. Soldiers remaining in service are treated within established military rehabilitation programs. If extensive treatment is indicated, they will be placed in Veterans Administration programs as facilities become available.

Tentative planning was completed to expand the identification and treatment program worldwide during the coming fiscal year. Although it is too early to assess the results of the relatively new programs, results achieved to date are promising and the effort has been well received by patients and by the civilian medical community.

Supplementing the medical aspects of the drug abuse correctional campaign, the Chief of Chaplains continued to conduct workshops (Ministry to the Drug User) emphasizing the moral and spiritual implications of the drug abuse.

Dissent

Soldier dissent and other antiwar and antimilitary activity directed against the Army continued to be a problem during fiscal year 1971. As in the past, the activities were analyzed and evaluated to see whether there was a co-ordinated central plan to undermine Army morale and discipline. Again, no new evidence appeared.

The number of known and suspected dissenters reported in the Army during the period decreased, while the number of those known to be involved in organizing, planning, or co-ordinating dissenting activity remained relatively stable. Manifestations of protest or dissent—demonstrations, organizational meetings, distribution of literature—fluctuated with the level of civil antiwar-antimilitary activity. Over-all, there was no indication that soldier dissent had been detrimental to combat effectiveness.

Conduct on the Battlefield

The legal consequences of alleged battlefield misconduct in operations around Son My (My Lai) in March 1968 continued during fiscal year 1971. Thirteen servicemen were charged with committing crimes against Vietnamese civilians at Son My, and twelve were charged with failure to properly investigate or report the incident. Of the thirteen charged, three were tried and acquitted, one was convicted, one was pending trial as the year closed, and charges against the others were dismissed. Of the twelve charged with failure to properly investigate or report the incident, one was pending trial, and adverse administrative action had been taken against two and was pending against five others. The charges were dismissed in all cases except the one pending trial.

In connection with battlefield misconduct, documents covering training in the Law of War were updated and new ones staffed, including lesson plans on war crimes and the duty to disobey criminal orders. Several training films on the Geneva and Hague conventions and enemy prisoners of war were also distributed.

Military Justice and Absenteeism

Since the enactment of the Military Justice Act of 1968, the Army has continued to improve the administration of military justice by regulatory changes not requiring legislation. As the statistics below indicate, most members of the Army who confront the military justice system do so at the level of nonjudicial punishment under Article 15 of the

Uniform Code of Military Justice. Article 15 provides for limited forms of punishment and is the lowest level of disciplinary action provided for by the code. A number of procedural changes have been made to improve the fairness of nonjudicial punishment. Notwithstanding the limited nature of the punishment permitted and the fact that such punishment does not become a permanent part of an individual's record, the Army has decided that each person facing punishment under Article 15 should be permitted to discuss his case with a lawyer before determining whether or not to accept punishment under Article 15. If an individual refuses punishment under Article 15, which he may do in all but very rare cases, he may face trial by court-martial, which involves the possibility of serious punishment and a permanent blot on his record. An individual should have the opportunity to discuss his case with a lawyer before making such a serious choice. Additionally, a service member may present defenses and matters in mitigation and extenuation to the officer imposing the punishment under Article 15, and a lawyer can aid the individual in preparing properly to present these matters. Procedures under Article 15 are designed to be as fair as possible consistent with the needs of discipline. The recent changes to the procedures should do much to improve the fairness of Article 15.

There were 45,736 persons tried by court-martial during fiscal year 1971, a rate of 35.73 per thousand, as compared with 58,999 in fiscal year 1970, a rate of 40.10 per thousand. The following chart compares totals and rates per thousand by type for fiscal years 1970 and 1971.

Type Court-martial	1970 Total	1970 Rate per 1,000	1971 Total	1971 Rate per 1,000
General	2,628	1.79	2,751	2.15
Special	41,348	28.07	27,989	21.87
Summary	15,023	10.20	14,996	11.71

In addition to these court-martial proceedings, 272,029 persons were punished under the provisions of Article 15 of the Uniform Code of Military Justice (212.5 per thousand), as compared with 318,200 in fiscal year 1970 (216 per thousand).

Under Article 86 of the code, 1,586 individuals were convicted by general court-martial for absence without leave (AWOL), as compared with 1,349 in the previous year. Under Article 85 of the code, 114 individuals were convicted by general court-martial for desertion, as compared with 185 in fiscal year 1970. Under special court-martial proceedings, bad conduct discharges were given to 862 individuals for absence without leave and to three individuals for desertion.

The Army developed several programs to reduce absenteeism. Seminars were conducted for small unit leaders to further their understanding of the AWOL and desertion problem. The supervision of all aspects of recovery operations was centralized at the department level, and the Continental Army Command sent assistance teams to personnel control facilities to establish procedures that would reduce the time required to process returnees.

There were 25,210 cases during the year ending November 30, 1970, in which members of the U.S. Army overseas were charged with offenses that were subject to the jurisdiction of foreign courts. In 11,800 of these cases, the offenses charged were solely violations of foreign law, and thus subject to exclusive foreign jurisdiction. The remaining 13,410 cases involved alleged violations of both United States military law and foreign law, over which the foreign country had the primary right to exercise jurisdiction. Foreign authorities waived their primary right to exercise jurisdiction in 12,481, or 93 percent, of these cases. Of the 10,801 members of the U.S. Army who were finally convicted by foreign courts only 66 received sentences to unsuspended confinement.

Misconduct off the Battlefield

During fiscal year 1971, the Permanent Subcommittee on Investigations of the Senate Committee on Government Operations resumed hearings and brought to light additional allegations of misconduct on the part of personnel concerned with the operation of clubs and open messes. At the time of these most recent hearings, the Army was already taking measures to improve the operations of the open mess system worldwide. Examples of action taken include creation of career patterns for noncommissioned and warrant officers assigned to manage open messes, initiation of a program for independent audit of open mess accounts by civilian accounting firms and the U.S. Army Audit Agency, promulgation of regulatory changes directed at improving internal fiscal control and supervision of open messes, and personal messages from the Chief of Staff to all major commanders stressing the importance of proper operation of these activities. Thorough and timely investigation of allegations of misconduct reveals that while instances of failures to implement regulatory control procedures are numerous, the vast majority of personnel concerned with the open mess system are honest, dedicated individuals and that dishonesty is limited to a few.

Race Relations

It has been a long-standing policy of the Army to conduct its activities free of racial discrimination, with equal opportunity and treatment for all members regardless of race, color, sex, religion, or national origin. Although great progress has been made in this regard, many problems remain, within the service as well as throughout society in general. Soldiers entering the Army bring with them the attitudes and beliefs that contribute to racial unrest in civilian communities. The Army has thus experienced some of the racial problems found in the larger society.

The Army has attempted to discover the root causes of racial discord and to emphasize the role of leadership in overcoming problems. The Army's goal is to insure that all soldiers are treated fairly and are afforded equal opportunity in all areas of Army life.

The Army has identified some problem areas in the race relations picture, among them ineffective communications between personnel of different ages and races; polarization of the races; a potential for group participation in racial incidents; a lack of timely information on the existence of tensions; and a lack of confidence among black soldiers in the promotion, redress, and judicial systems. The need for more effective measures to reduce racial conflict is recognized, however, and the Army has acted on a number of counts to assure racial harmony within its ranks. Army combat readiness has not been impaired by internal racial friction. Yet even a minor amount of racial unrest and incident is undesirable on any basis, and the Army has moved along many lines to further racial harmony. In the last year, instruction in race relations was incorporated into the Army educational system. Under Continental Army Command direction, the U.S. Army Infantry School at Fort Benning, Georgia, developed and tested a course, and a four-hour block of instruction was included in the curriculum for junior leaders at Army service schools beginning in September 1970. The instruction is designed to develop among commissioned officers, warrant officers, and noncommissioned officers an understanding of the basic factors in race relations, the causes of racial tension, and measures to foster racial harmony. The Infantry School also developed a course for presentation in basic combat training; it was tested at Fort Jackson, South Carolina, in November 1970 and introduced in all training centers in January 1971. Other race relations training was developed within major Army commands.

An Army-wide Race Relations Conference was held during the period of November 17–20, 1970, to examine systematically the racial problems facing the armed forces, to exchange information on positive measures developed by Army commanders to resolve racial problems, and to develop recommendations for future programs to improve the racial climate.

Steps were also taken during the year to make the Army Exchange System more responsive to the needs and preferences of minority group personnel, and a similar action was taken in the selection of literature for Army libraries worldwide.

Discrimination in off-post housing, one of the more serious problems in racial relations, continued to plague the minority group soldier and his family at home and abroad. A number of new Army procedures were instituted to get at the root of this problem. All Army members, for example, whether overseas or in the United States, are required to process through a housing referral office before entering into a rental or lease agreement. In turn, housing referral offices worldwide now require agents and owners to sign unqualified assurances that they will rent or lease their facilities without regard to race, under the basic policy that a facility is either open to all soldiers or will be open to none. Commanders were instructed to impose restrictive sanctions upon any rental facility whose owner or agent discriminates against military personnel. Furthermore, the internal operations and staffing of all Army housing referral offices were examined to insure that the Army's nondiscriminatory policies were being followed.

The Army also instituted special recruiting programs for minority group officers, and, as the year closed, these efforts were beginning to show positive results. Most noteworthy was the upward mobility of Negro officers during the period of this report. One active Army Negro officer was promoted to major general and three were nominated for promotion to brigadier general. Two Reserve Component Negro officers were promoted to brigadier general.

Intelligence Policy

Over the past several years a considerable amount of attention has been centered on the Army's civil intelligence collection operations and the degree to which such activity infringes on the constitutional rights of the citizen. As early as February 5, 1969, the Under Secretary of the Army expressed concern that intelligence collection activities related to civil disturbance problems might exceed strict requirements and intrude upon areas that were essentially of civilian concern. A memorandum of that date directed that, in the collection of civil disturbance information, primary reliance should be placed upon liaison with local, state, and federal law enforcement agencies, and that a quarterly report of U.S. Army Intelligence Command overt collection activities other than through normal liaison should be provided. This memorandum also prohibited covert collection operations unless concurred in by the Federal Bureau of Investigation and approved in advance by the Under Secretary of the Army.

Actions to implement this memorandum included the publication of two letters of instruction. One, published on April 1, 1970, directed that no intelligence data bank related to civil disturbance or other activities concerning civilians not affiliated with the Department of Defense would be instituted or retained without the approval of the Secretary of the Army and the Chief of Staff. The second letter, issued on June 9, 1970, restricted the Army from gathering civil disturbance information until the Department of Justice issues a warning of a disturbance that may exceed civil law enforcement capabilities.

The continuing review of Army counterintelligence activities to insure that they are consistent with constitutional rights while meeting national security needs led to the publication on December 15, 1970, of another departmental letter, listing the types of situations that represent a threat to the Army and warrant intelligence collection, and prohibiting the collection and storage of other information pertaining to civilians not affiliated with the Department of Defense. This letter also directed that existing files be purged of all information not authorized by the letter.

On December 23, 1970, the Secretary of Defense issued a memorandum to the secretaries of the military departments, the Chairman of the Joint Chiefs of Staff, and the directors of defense agencies, stating his desire to be certain that Defense Department intelligence and counterintelligence activities were completely consistent with constitutional rights, other legal provisions, and national security needs. He stressed that these activities must be conducted in a manner that recognizes and preserves individual rights, and that policy determinations governing such activities must be retained under civilian guidance and control. This memorandum led to the publication of two Department of Defense directives providing for senior civilian cognizance and control over the Defense Investigative Program and formalizing certain organizational and procedural steps for the program. On June 1, 1971, the Army issued an implementing letter restating Army policy and providing direction concerning the collection, reporting, processing, and storage of information on civilians or civilian organizations not affiliated with the Department of Defense.

VII. Reserve Forces

The reserve forces of the Army consist of the Army National Guard (ARNG) and the U.S. Army Reserve (USAR). Known collectively as the Reserve Components, their mission is to provide trained units and qualified individuals for active duty in time of war or national emergency. The National Guard has two additional missions: to participate full-time in the air defense of the nation, and to provide units that are organized, equipped, and trained to function efficiently under federal or state authority in order to protect life and property and preserve peace, order, and public safety.

The Reserve Component force structure in fiscal year 1971 consisted of eight combat divisions, twenty-one separate brigades, and enough units to round out the active Army's division forces and provide balanced division forces in the Reserve Components. Because of constant commitments and requirements, contraction of the active Army, and increasing dependence upon backup forces, the priorities of the Reserve Components have risen. The assignment of early missions for many units has improved unit spirit and sense of mission. There has also been a growing rapport and understanding between the Reserve Components and the active Army.

Readiness

Several steps were taken to further the Reserve Components' ability to operate in the modern Army environment, to insure compatibility with active Army organization, operation, and doctrine. Conversion of the Reserve Components to the latest active Army tables of organization and equipment was begun in early deployment units and will progress through the remainder of the structure during fiscal year 1972. Concurrently, the force structure was reviewed and refinements to adapt it to the total force were initiated. Units no longer required are to be eliminated, and the new troop structure will be incorporated in the modernized "One Army" force.

There was progress in the Reserve Components' aviation program during the year, in aircraft deliveries, aviator and technical personnel recruiting and training, and the preparation of units to receive aircraft. A growing airlift capability is enhancing the training of maneuver units in airmobile exercises and will make aviation assets available to active Army units located near Reserve Component elements.

Missile systems are a growing part of the reserve force. Issue of the Sheridan armored airborne assault vehicle equipped with the Shillelagh missile system was initiated to one of the higher priority Reserve Component units, and Redeye training will begin soon in anticipation of receipt of weapons. Prospects for issue of the Dragon missile system are good; Honest John will remain in the inventory indefinitely.

Reserve Component units and individuals participated in several active Army exercises in the past year.

Personnel

The Reserve Components have been able to maintain mandated strength in the conscription environment, but the absence of the draft will affect recruitment in the reserves. An analysis of the random sequence birthdate groups for enlistees with no prior service in the Army Reserve Components during the first quarter of fiscal year 1971 revealed that between 77 and 91 percent of enlistments were draft-motivated. Studies indicate that productive enlistment and retention incentives will be needed if Reserve Component strength is to be maintained after the draft is eliminated. Thus volunteer Army programs will be adapted to the Reserve Components. Both low-cost and no-cost incentives will be used to encourage volunteers.

The Army continued to implement recommendations of a special board to improve the management of the Reserve Component officer corps. Of 99 recommendations, 84 were completed, 9 deleted, 3 deferred, and 3 requiring legislation were under consideration by the House Armed Services Committee.

The fiscal year 1971 Defense Authorization Act prescribed an average paid drill strength of not less than 400,000 in ARNG units and 260,000 in USAR units. When applied to the Reserve Component troop structure, this arrangement permits units to be manned at over 90 percent of authorized strength. The actual average strength of the components during the year was 400,842 for the National Guard and 261,521 for the Army Reserve.

Enlisted accessions in units during the year totaled 52,425 enlistees with no prior service and 13,133 with prior service in the National Guard, and 30,175 enlistees with no prior service and 8,027 with prior service in the Army Reserve.

The individual training status of both components in fiscal year 1971 was as follows:

	ARNG	USAR	Total
Assigned strengths	402,175	263,299	665,474
REP awaiting training	16,802	7,315	24,117
REP in training	26,787	17,843	44,630
REP training completed in fiscal year	84,652	30,271	114,923
Trained strength	358,586	238,141	596,727
Percent of assigned trained	89.2	90.4	89.7

There was considerable progress in Reserve Enlistment Program (REP) training during the year. Those REP candidates awaiting training were reduced from 52,222 as the year opened to 24,117 as the year closed. The availability of additional spaces in the Army training base permitted the Reserve Components to enter 18,000 more REP candidates in training than had been programed. Beginning in March 1971, trainees from early deployment units had equal priority with active Army personnel for training spaces. By the end of the year, no Reserve Enlistment Program men of early deployment units who were awaiting training had been delayed more than ninety days.

The number of Reserve Component technicians decreased during the fiscal year from 29,899 to 29,773. The number of technicians increased in all activities except on-site defense, where Nike-Hercules deployment decreased. The following table depicts the status of ARNG and USAR technicians at the close of the year:

	ARNG	USAR	Total
Required	27,283	7,066	34,349
Programed	24,249	6,427	30,676
Assigned	23,273	6,500	29,773

Adoption of new selection criteria for assignment of active Army officers as advisers to Reserve Component units has improved the quality of advice. Adviser status at the end of the fiscal year was as follows:

	ARNG	USAR	Total
Officers			
Authorized	859	755	1,614
Assigned	655	702	1,357
Enlisted			
Authorized	1,186	1,230	2,416
Assigned	1,100	1,140	2,240

The Individual Ready Reserve (IRR) of the USAR is comprised of Ready Reservists who are not members of units. They are assigned to five control groups, as described in detail in last year's report. In the past year they were assigned, by category, as follows:

Control Group	Officers	Enlisted	Total
Annual training	22,665	683,754	706,419
Mobilization designation	4,601		4,601
Reinforcement	25,602	236,346	261,948
Delayed	0	15	15
Officer active duty obligor	18,000	2	18,002
Total	70,868	920,117	990,985

Materiel and Supply

Fiscal year 1971 was a banner period for the issue and modernization of equipment for the Reserve Components. Equipment valued at $727 million was issued to units, well above the $150 million and $300 million issued respectively in the two previous years. Enough rifles were received so that all combat units could be equipped with the M16 and other units with the M16 and M14. Thus the Reserve Components are now equipped with the same rifles as the active Army. The M14 will be gradually phased out as more M16 rifles become available.

Approximately two hundred M–60 tanks were distributed to the reserve forces in fiscal year 1971 to meet training needs, supplementing the M–48 series models. Early deployment units will receive full training allowances before the close of fiscal year 1972. Issue of a new family of tactical radios was also initiated. Increased quantities of wheeled vehicles, some direct from manufacturers, were also issued. First-line aircraft were received, including CH–47, CH–54, and UH–1D helicopters. Older models were being withdrawn and replaced, so that during the year the Reserve Component fleet increased from 933 to 1,353 aircraft and was being markedly upgraded in quality.

Although there will continue to be equipment shortages, all early deploying combat units will be equipped to a level of about 80 percent of organizational equipment by the middle of fiscal year 1972, while all others in that category (up to mobilization plus ninety days) will meet that goal by the close of the next fiscal year, and the equipment status of those to deploy after M+90 will be improved.

Now that equipment is becoming available at an accelerated rate, Reserve Component units are following the same requisitioning system used by active Army units, requesting authorized equipment as needed, with the Department of the Army controlling items in short supply. All Reserve Component units cannot, of course, use, store, or maintain full levels of equipment in a premobilization status. In such a situation a unit is issued the amount of equipment—approximately 80 percent of the full allowance—to support training at its home station during weekend drills and at annual training sites. Postmobilization requirements include the additional stocks that would bring the units to full wartime authorization and provide pipeline, maintenance, and combat stocks.

Logistic management received major attention during the year under programs to control the distribution of priority materiel and equipment. A maintenance program was initiated to repair inoperable equipment, including tanks, aircraft, personnel carriers, and communications equipment, and a test program was undertaken by the National Guard to repair unserviceable vehicles from Vietnam in ARNG maintenance shops. The test is unique because the Guard is providing the labor and repairing equipment with parts supplied by the active Army. Over two hundred trucks were programed for shipment to ARNG shops in Virginia, California, and Mississippi, to be repaired and issued to ARNG units. The program will be extended to include about one thousand armored personnel carriers from Europe. The Reserve Components were also designated to receive some reconditioned equipment from Vietnam.

Depot stockage procedures were reviewed to insure that early deploying units can be provided with equipment required to raise them from the 80-percent level to full authorization. With the phase-down of the active Army and the liquidation of the Vietnam War, equipment forecasts for the Reserve Components are excellent. Relatively small inventories and limited procurement of some items, however, mean that some major equipment shortages will continue despite accelerated issues.

Installations and Facilities

Reserve Component facility construction requirements are determined by the approved mandated force structure, the stationing of units within the structure based on manpower potential within the several states, and the condition of existing facilities in which units are housed.

At present, all Reserve Component units occupy some type of facility. However, these facilities range from permanently constructed National Guard armories and Army Reserve centers to leased structures of varying adequacy. The current Reserve Component real property inventory is valued at $907.4 million, of which $648 million is in Army National Guard facilities and $259.4 million in Army Reserve facilities.

While the over-all preparedness of the Reserve Components is probably the highest ever achieved in peacetime, sufficient resources to maintain the highest possible level of proficiency must be available. A fundamental resource requirement is availability of adequate, functional, self-sustaining facilities.

To provide essential home station facilities and training areas to meet the current force structure, improve unit training capability, promote unit readiness, and enhance esprit de corps and morale, a ten-year military construction plan was developed, identifying facility requirements totaling $639.7 million. Of this amount, $301.3 million would provide for Army National Guard facilities and $338.4 million for the Army Reserve. The goal of this construction plan is to provide adequate facilities for all units by 1980. The Deputy Secretary of Defense approved the concept in January 1970. The first five years of the plan provided $25 million in fiscal year 1971 and $55 million per year in fiscal years 1972 through 1975. The residual deficiency will be programed over the remaining five years. As fiscal year 1971 was the initial construction year of the program, the budget plan provided a new obligational authority of $25 million for military construction. Therefore, the funding available to support the Reserve Component fiscal year 1971 construction increment was as follows:

Fund Category	ARNG	USAR
	(in millions of dollars)	
New obligational authority	15.0	10.0
Prior-year funds available	6.3	13.2
Funds available	21.3	23.2
Funds obligated	16.4	11.6
Carry-over for fiscal year 1972	4.9	11.6

With available funding, the Army National Guard was authorized construction of thirty armories at a estimated federal cost of $7.85 million. The Army Reserve program provided for eleven new centers and two center expansions at an estimated cost of $9.29 million. The status of armory and center facility requirements as of end fiscal year 1971 was as follows:

	Required	Occupied	Adequate	Requirements[a]
ARNG	2744	2744	2038	706
USAR	1019	1019	225	794

[a] Fifteen hundred armories and centers require replacement, expansion, conversion, or rehabilitation of existing facilities to meet revised space criteria.

In addition, thirty-two nonarmory facilities, which provide administrative and logistical support to Reserve Component units, were authorized for the National Guard at an estimated cost of $5.89 million. The Army Reserve does not fund separately for this type of facility, since such requirements are constructed as part of a reserve center. Of the 2,479 nonarmory (administrative and logistical) facilities that support the National Guard, 2,254 are considered adequate. The remaining 225 require replacement, expansion, or alteration to correct certain deficiencies at a cost of $52.6 million.

The lack of adequate training areas continues to be a constraint on operational readiness. A survey of all 402 combat and combat support battalions was completed in April 1970. This survey revealed that 39 percent of the battalions examined have adequate training sites. An analysis of the survey identified 224 units with specific training area needs that must be satisfied. Of these, 146 units have been given recommended courses of action in overcoming deficiencies; 53 have reported that their problems have been resolved; and there are indications that more units are satisfying their needs through adjustment of training schedules and the utilization of training areas within reasonable commuting distances of the home stations that were not previously considered. Recommendations for correcting deficiencies in the remaining 78 units will be addressed after specific inactive duty training requirements for certain combat support battalions have been determined.

Base closures provide an excellent source of training area acquisitions for the Reserve Components. Reports of excess posts are closely screened, and areas which could satisfy training requirements are identified and reported to the General Services Administration for licensing to the Reserve Component that requested primary use of the site. The Army National Guard's programed construction of training facilities at ten federal- and state-owned or -controlled installations during fiscal year 1971 was increased from $2.57 million to $5.22 million. Backlogs of construction at the federal and state camps amount to $44.6 million for the National Guard. The Army Reserve training area requirement amounts to $28 million. As the funding levels of the military construction programs increase in the final years of the ten-year construction plan, emphasis can be placed on increased funding for construction at weekend and annual training sites.

Training

The premobilization training objective for most Reserve Component units is to attain and maintain company-level proficiency, which is verified by the successful completion of an appropriate Army training test. Some units have met this objective. Several constraints, however, work against the Reserve Components as they endeavor to reach their premobilization objectives. These are equipment shortages, limited areas available for tactical training, and insufficient training time. Further increase in training time allocations also affects the budget, as personnel costs make up a large percentage of expenditures. Equipment shortages and training area limitations were being improved at a rapid rate and are becoming less of a problem now than in previous years.

Clearly defined primary and alternate missions with readiness objectives based on operational requirements are given to Reserve Component units. The purpose is to provide a high level of motivation by insuring the commander's awareness of the importance of his role. Mission assignments are to be disseminated to all commanders down to and including separate company, platoon, and detachment levels and are to include the unit's mobilization station, readiness objective, employment-deployment mission, and area of orientation.

To capitalize on the limited training time available, several innovative programs were under way that promise to bring improved training to Reserve Component units.

The Program for Improving Readiness includes an associate unit concept involving the alignment of Reserve Component units with similar units of the active Army; a system that rounds out active Army combat units to their deployment configurations using Reserve Component units; an addition of technicians to units in order to evaluate the impact on unit readiness; and an evaluation of the recovery time required for reconstruction of a unit upon demobilization. Also included is a test of the feasibility of Reserve Component participation in active Army exercises and another test to determine the feasibility of moving into advanced unit training when a unit achieves the objective of company-level proficiency.

The Mutual Support Program is an effort to expand the associated unit idea to Army-wide application. It consists of jointly operated programs of self-help between active and Reserve Component forces. Significant growth is anticipated with the imminent publication of an Army regulation on this matter. These first two programs have resulted, in the early stages of their development, in improved individual proficiency in Reserve Component units. As further development occurs, advances in unit training status are expected to become more apparent.

The Intensive Management Program is designed to provide close management of Reserve Component assets for the early deployment units, and to provide high-level officials with information on the status of those units. Despite early difficulty in establishing an adequate data base, the program promises to become a valuable tool of management for units that must meet deployment schedules not previously required of Reserve Component units.

With continued deliveries of modern equipment and increased availability of adequate training areas, the outlook for improved training levels is good.

Management

Continued use of the Ten Point Improvement Program as a management tool for the Reserve Components highlighted problems for corrective action and led to such accomplishments as those outlined above. Under the impetus of the program, Reserve Component units have received an increasing number of visits by high-ranking representatives of the military departments, and major staff agencies have designated contact points for Reserve Component affairs. Public Affairs Program coverage of the Reserve Components was expanded through audio-visual and publications activities, briefings, visits, and awards.

Automatic data processing (ADP) entered the Reserve Component picture when the Consolidated Reserve Component Automated Personnel System became operational in September 1970, and Army-owned ADP equipment was acquired for Reserve Component brigades. Equipment for Reserve Component brigades was earmarked for two units of the ARNG and USAR; after testing the prototype units this number will be expanded to fifteen brigade-size units. Creation of a Reserve Components Army Aviation Committee in August 1970 to advise on the development of a sound aviation program assures consideration and planning for this type of equipment in the aviation area.

Military Support to Civil Authorities

During the year, 16,668 National Guardsmen were called by their governors to state active duty for civil disturbance emergencies. These Guardsmen were used forty-three times in twenty-two states to assist civil authorities in quelling civil disturbances in cities and on campuses. National Guard forces were also ordered to state active duty seventy-seven times in thirty states to assist civil authorities during natural disasters and other emergencies. These call-ups included rescue operations during blizzards and floods; security, traffic control, and evacuation during tornadoes and hurricanes; searches for missing persons and downed aircraft; water-hauls in drought areas; air-drops of food to snowbound cattle; and forest fire control.

The ability of the National Guard to conduct operations in controlling civil disturbances was increased during fiscal year 1971. This improvement was a result of civil disturbance training, the purchase of civil disturbance control equipment, and improved planning at the state level.

In addition to the sixteen hours of annual civil disturbance refresher training conducted by Army National Guard units in past years, all units with specific civil disturbance missions completed an extra eight hours of refresher training during the period April 1–June 30, 1971. Key noncommissioned officers and junior officers in the grade of lieutenant and captain holding leadership positions in units with a civil disturbance mission received a special sixteen-hour course of leadership instruction, designed to provide increased command and control capabilities in company-size units committed to any future civil disturbance control operation. The program of instruction and lesson plans were developed by the active Army and the instruction was executed by the adjutant general of each state, using experienced instructors. The Army National Guard provided instructors and instructional material to the Air National Guard in order to initiate training of designated Air Guard units and individuals in civil disturbance control operations.

Funds were made available within the Army budget to purchase 137,598 face shields, 136,737 riot batons, and 111,244 protective vests. The face shields and riot batons were in the hands of National Guard units throughout the fifty states, the District of Columbia, and the commonwealth of Puerto Rico. The protective vests were being shipped to the states. Through co-ordination with the Army Materiel Command, XM33 riot control agent dispersers were being placed in National Guard units, and "low-lethality" items such as the baseball grenade were available to Guardsmen. The Army National Guard co-operated with the Office, Chief of Research and Development, in evaluating the plastic, disposable, flexible handcuff for use in mass detention situations during civil disturbance control operations.

The civil disturbance plans of each state were examined in detail by a special panel of military support experts. The findings of this study group were then reviewed by a special committee of six adjutants general who met in the Pentagon on December 1–2, 1970. This committee submitted specific recommendations which were then passed to the states under personal letter to each adjutant general. As a result of this action, fifty states, the District of Columbia, and the commonwealth of Puerto Rico agreed to standardize their civil disturbance planning and to adopt the Federal Rules for Application of Force.

During fiscal year 1971 a communications study group was convened to survey Guard communication needs based on civil disturbance control. The study fixed the status of communications and recommendations for standardization and improvement. A selected group of military support plans officers reviewed the study, and final recommendations will become policy matters for implementation in fiscal year 1972.

During the fiscal year, 403 National Guard officers attended the civil disturbance orientation course at the Military Police School, Fort Gordon, Georgia, and 275 National Guard officers were programed to attend during fiscal year 1972.

The National Guard Bureau participated in a Department of the Army civil disturbance study during this fiscal year. Many of the actions taken to improve civil disturbance training and equipment stem from this study. The exchange of ideas and the co-operative efforts demonstrated during the course of the study were of mutual benefit to the National Guard and the active Army.

Members of the Office of Military Support to Civil Authorities visited thirty-six states, the District of Columbia, and Puerto Rico during the year to observe civil disturbance training and command post exercises, to assist in the preparation of civil disturbance operations plans, and to participate in civil defense conferences or seminars and related aspects of the military support field.

VIII. Management, Budget, and Funds

Management is the process of establishing and attaining objectives to carry out responsibilities. It consists of the variety of continuing actions that are required to plan, organize, co-ordinate, control, and evaluate the use of men, money, and materials to accomplish missions and tasks.

Organizational Developments

There were several organizational developments during the fiscal year that were of some significance. At the department level the importance of the shift away from dependence upon the draft and toward a volunteer Army was recognized with the designation by the Chief of Staff, on October 28, 1970, of the Special Assistant for the Modern Volunteer Army (SAMVA). Three days later this special assistant was issued a charter outlining his mission under the Modern Volunteer Army Program: to establish conditions that would contribute to the effectiveness of the Army while reducing reliance on the draft; to raise the number and quality of enlistments and re-enlistments; to promote service attractiveness and career motivation; and to provide for a standby draft law to meet national emergencies. The SAMVA office developed a program for the modern volunteer army outlining actions, incentives, priorities, requirements, experiments, funding, and goals for fiscal years 1971 and 1972.

For the second time within a five-year period, two of the continental armies were merged. As the year closed, the Fourth and Fifth U.S. Armies were consolidated, and their headquarters merged as the Fifth U.S. Army at Fort Sam Houston, Texas. The Fourth Army was inactivated effective June 30, 1971, and the Fifth Army became responsible for an area embracing fourteen states (see chapter 2), while activities in Colorado, the Dakotas, and Wyoming were transferred to the Sixth Army at San Francisco.

Another organizational move grew out of the recommendations of the Special Review (Parker) Panel on Department of the Army Reorganization. Noting that the Military District of Washington (MDW), because of its location and special mission as a headquarters command for the Department of the Army, deals directly with the department and other government agencies in the national capital region, the Parker Panel recommended that the Continental Army Command (CONARC) be relieved of command responsibility for MDW.

On May 22, 1971, a plan was approved under which MDW would become a major Army field command effective July 1, 1971, reporting directly to Headquarters, Department of the Army.

Management Programs and Systems

During fiscal year 1971 the master plan for Army management systems was revised to provide a basic tool for controlling the development, evolution, and operation of Army management systems through the five-year period from 1972 through 1976. The plan will insure that an approved and defensible basis exists for management information systems planning, programing, budgeting, and resource allocation.

A number of automatic data processing systems progressed during the year. The Base Operating System (BASOPSO), the Army's first multicommand and multifunctional computer system, was operating at fourteen CONARC installations as the year closed. It is designed to meet managing and reporting requirements at the installation level and to standardize computer applications and procedures, not only in CONARC but at oversea installations as well. The initial applications are military personnel accounting, supply, and finance.

The first phase of the Army Materiel Command Logistics Program Hardcore Automated (ALPHA) became operational on May 1, 1971. This program is a standard system for the wholesale inventory management operation at the commodity command level within the Army Materiel Command; later phases are to be completed by January 1972 at the prototype installation, the Aviation Systems Command at St. Louis, Missouri.

Conversion from the service number to the social security number for identification of military personnel increased the need for effective controls over registration, correction, and changes in names and social security numbers throughout the Department of Defense, especially in automated data files. The Army was directed to develop a social security number (SSN) verification procedure to be used by all the services. The procedure, known in the Army as the Social Security Number Central Registry System, verifies social security numbers through comparison with the automated individual records of the Social Security Administration. This comparison, in conjunction with other internal Army controls imposed under the Central Registry System, will increase the accuracy of SSN data. Agreements concerning verification procedures were reached with the Social Security Administration, and verification of the social security numbers with Army personnel and finance systems proceeded during the year.

Modern computer technology and management practices were also applied to the development during the year of a number of new personnel models that would provide more accurate and timely personnel information. Among the areas addressed were the Comparison of Manpower Programs using Linear Programming (COMPLIP), a model to estimate the number of personnel projected to be in the Army's trained strength, basic and advanced individual training programs, and the Reserve Enlistment Program; the Personnel Inventory Analysis (PIA), a model to provide management planners with a means to project the status of the Army's personnel inventory as related to force structure; the Student Instructor Load (SIL), a model to predict the number of students that will enter Army service schools; the Military Personnel Army Budget Models Program, to cover six elements of personnel activity; the Simulation of Personnel Operation (SIMPO), a series of models to simulate policies and operations of the personnel system; and the Data Element Cost Model, to estimate acquisition and maintenance data costs.

The systemwide project for electronic equipment at depots extended (SPEEDEX), an information system for use at continental U.S. Army Materiel Command depots, was operational during the year at the Letterkenny Army Depot at Chambersburg, Pennsylvania. Approval was given in February 1971 to extend it to two additional depots. The system is being designed by the Materiel Command's Logistics System Support Agency.

Another ongoing program in the logistic field was the USARPAC Standard Supply System, a theater depot and inventory control center for supply and related financial data processing. During fiscal year 1971, RCA Spectra 70 computers were selected to replace existing IBM equipment at six locations within U.S. Army, Pacific. An evaluation of the prototype installation in Hawaii was completed in June 1971, and the new computers will be installed at the other sites during fiscal year 1972.

The automated system for Army commissaries, which would mechanize nine basic commissary applications at the installation level, progressed during the year. Concepts were developed and tested at field installations during 1966–1967 and were developed by contractors during 1970. Prototype testing by the Army Materiel Command and the Continental Army Command was completed at 2 installations in May 1971, and the system is scheduled to be installed at 101 installations Army-wide during fiscal year 1972.

The Corps of Engineers Management Information System (COEMIS), to standardize comptroller, personnel, resource allocation, and real estate management in engineer division and districts in the continental United States, completed prototype application in the South Pacific division at San Francisco, California, during the year and on May 6, 1971, was approved for extension to the eight other division centers, beginning with the North Central division at Chicago, Illinois, in December 1971.

In Europe, the operating system of the military districts of the U.S. Theater Army Support Command embraces four major subsystems —logistical management, financial management, maintenance management, and property book. During the year, steps were under way to replace leased equipment with government-owned equipment at seven installations. Test equipment was installed in April 1971 at the Sued Bayern district.

During the year division-level Combat Service Support System (CS3) completed prototype testing at Fort Hood, Texas. The system provides an Army-wide standardized and automated logistics, personnel, and administrative system for Army division support. As the year closed, work was in progress to correct certain deficiences revealed by the test, and a study had been completed to determine manpower requirements.

The Department of Defense Integrated Management Engineering Systems (DIMES) review schedule for fiscal year 1971 included seven Army activities. A joint service DIMES implementation review at Sharpe Army Depot, California, in September 1970 was the first comprehensive appraisal within the Army with primary attention centered on management use of work measurement standards in work planning and control, manpower, and budget determinations. A number of problems were identified. The Army Materiel Command developed a plan that would respond to recommendations for corrective action. Four priority areas were established which would be covered by standards by the end of the fiscal year: supply, supply management, maintenance, and base accounts. The Army Materiel Command plan was forwarded to all field commands as a model to be followed in implementing DIMES. All other DIMES reviews were canceled.

Activities continued under the Logistics Performance Measurement and Evaluation System (LPMES) during the year. Established in 1969 as a means by which to concentrate management improvement actions on persistent problems in the logistics field, the LPMES expresses performance in units, percentages, dollars, items, and other terms applicable to an area under consideration, with comparisons made against a base period and established goals. Seventeen problem areas were under system management during the year, paced by ninety-two performance indicators; thirty-three of these were considered to be primary, with corrective action to be completed in fiscal year 1971.

A comprehensive study of the policies and principles of interservice, interdepartmental, and interagency support was completed during the past fiscal year. In implementing study recommendations, the Army emphasized the cost benefits to be realized through this kind of support. As the year closed the Army was participating in a multiservice effort to develop joint regulations that would permit installation commanders to respond more effectively to requests for interservice support.

The Army, indeed, has taken a leading role in proposing Defense-wide policies and in negotiating and executing interservice agreements in the field of common logistics support. The Army has proposed that resources allocated to common logistics support arrangements be fully recognized within the program-budget process; that expansion of common logistics support arrangements be premised on efficiency and economy; that existing roles and missions be changed to further interservice support relationships; and that any logistic function performed within the Department of Defense be assigned to one component as a mission responsibility for support of all others. This approach was presented in April 1971 to the Military Logistics Council, and an *ad hoc* group formed by that body concluded that retail interservice support should be the initial area in which to expand common logistic support arrangements, using as a medium the Defense Retail Interservice Logistic Support (DRILS) program.

The Army Commercial and Industrial Activities Program was an important vehicle during the year in the search for efficient and economical ways of carrying out Army functions under increasingly austere conditions. Because of fund and manpower constraints, major commands appraised functions and performance alternatives to determine ways to save money. In some cases, operational changes sparked both local and national interest because of personnel reductions or contract terminations.

During the fiscal year a civilian career program for transportation management was established. It will provide an orderly input of interns, a formal training plan for all career levels, and a career referral system for selection of candidates to fill vacant transportation positions Army-wide. Also during the year a Department of the Army career planning board met and recommended an expansion of the present Equipment Specialist Civilian Career Program into a comprehensive Materiel Maintenance Management Career Program. The program incorporates formal intern recruitment and training that will enable the department to narrow the age and education gap that now exists in the maintenance management work force.

The report of survey covering lost, damaged, or destroyed property was reviewed during the year, and a number of changes were made to reduce manpower requirements and facilitate the processing of surveys. Under new procedures, a report of survey will not be required in order to waive accountability for lost or damaged organizational property nor will an individual be held financially liable and be required to pay for it. A commanding officer will be authorized to sign a certificate stating that the property may be dropped from accountability, and he will rely upon the Uniform Code of Military Justice to punish the individual causing the loss or damage if it was the result of negligence or misconduct. There are, however, because of statutory requirements, two situations under which reports of survey may be required. When a service member loses or damages his personal arms or equipment and does not admit liability, a report of survey is necessary before he can be held financially liable. In the case of shortages in the accounts of an officer who is accountable for government property, an investigation by a board of officers or a report of survey is necessary to determine liability.

In June 1970 the Bureau of the Budget initiated a government-wide effort to improve federal reporting and reduce related paperwork. In August the President established an over-all savings goal of $200 million, and while no specific goal was set for the Army, a savings of some $25 million was anticipated. Under the Army element of the program, called Project SAVER (Study to Assess and Validate Essential Reports), reports were reviewed worldwide and decisions were made to rescind, revise, or consolidate requirements at department headquarters, with estimated savings of $27.1 million. Army field command savings amounted to another $8.9 million.

To improve management practices in military units, a new instructional program for first-line supervisors—junior officers, warrant officers, and noncommissioned officers—was begun during fiscal year 1971. The program provides for instruction in methods improvement, work measurement, quality control, soldier motivation, and the management process. A pilot test was conducted in the 1st Infantry Division (Mechanized), and by year's end the training had been completed in the 82d Airborne Division and at Fort Hood, Texas. The program will be included in the curricula of Army service schools and the Command and General Staff College as well as in unit training programs.

A review of the impact of inspections, reporting requirements, and fund solicitations on morale and mission accomplishment in military units indicated that the average company- and battalion-size unit expends from 20 to 33 percent of usable unit effort meeting inspection and reporting requirements. The results of the review were circulated throughout the Army Staff to be used in connection with Modern Volunteer Army Program actions.

In fiscal year 1971 the use of analytical studies as an aid in resource allocation continued to increase. Economic analysis was especially helpful in improving resource allocation, in evaluating proposed ADP systems, in ordering priorities for major construction, and in improving the efficiency of the Production Base Support Program.

The Army also continued to rely heavily upon cost analysis to evaluate alternatives among weapon systems and force structures. In addition to conducting continuing reviews of cost estimates for weapon, support, communications, and aircraft systems, cost analysts were called upon regularly to assist in the intensified planning required by force reductions and growing fiscal constraints. Studies were undertaken to determine what portion of the Army's total obligation authority was being allocated to certain systems such as aviation, combat vehicles, and artillery. A handbook of cost methodology and procedures was published, and other handbooks were being written to provide standardized factors for use in preparing or evaluating cost estimates of both materiel and forces.

A Mark Twain Financial Information System was developed during the year, capable of displaying financial resources data in a variety of formats. The system will be a valuable tool for support of major exercises in the planning, programing, and budgeting system. Also developed during the year was a cost model for use in the Strategic Forces Options 83, with an ability to accommodate time-phasing, address triservice costs, and display cost data according to major function and fiscal guidance categories.

Continued emphasis has been placed on the improvement and analysis of selected acquisition reports. These reports serve as a management tool to bring problems to the surface and focus attention on matters requiring decisions by top management on major Army weapon and support systems.

As the year closed the Army was preparing to convert to the Joint Uniform Military Pay System. Military pay personnel in the finance system were being trained through the year, old pay files were being purified, and tests were being made of the computers and programs. The new military pay system will go into effect for U.S. Army personnel in the continental United States in August; in Europe and Africa in October; and in the Pacific, Alaska, and Panama in November 1971. The cost of development, test, and first-year operations will be more than paid for in the first year of operation of the more efficient, centrally controlled system.

Budget and Funds

The Army's budget request for regular appropriations for fiscal year 1971 totaled $23,300.5 million in new obligational authority. Following reviews by the Office of the Secretary of Defense and the Bureau of the Budget, the President requested $20,943.7 million for the Army, and the Congress appropriated $20,301.1 million. The chronological development of this budget is traced in the accompanying table.

The fiscal year 1971 column of the fiscal year 1972 budget originally included $701.9 million for military and civilian pay raises effective December 27, 1969, and for wage board and foreign national increases anticipated through June 30, 1971. Subsequently, this amount was increased to $1,060.7 million due to an additional supplemental request (HR92–73, March 23, 1971) for military and civilian pay raises effective January 1, 1971, and for wage board increases resulting from the Monroney Amendment.

Resources Conservation Program

Beginning with fiscal year 1971 the Army Cost Reduction Program was redesignated the Army Resources Conservation Program in line with policy and procedural changes in the over-all Department of Defense program. Several major changes were made in the program in order to reduce paperwork and administrative work load and to increase motivation and participation.

On January 30, 1971, the Office of the Secretary of Defense canceled its instruction on the Resources Conservation Program and assigned responsibility to the military departments and the Defense Supply Agency for complying with the Office of Management and Budget Circular A–44, "Establishment of a Management Improvement Program applicable to all Government Operations," one element of which is cost reduction. This assignment is in line with the current Secretary of Defense policy to decentralize the operative aspects of program management to the individual services.

Under its new authority, the Army announced changes in the program, such as the modification of certain rules which previously precluded acceptance of savings actions, and the assignment of responsibility for assuring the validity of savings to commanders instead of the U.S. Army Audit Agency.

The 1st Logistical Command, U.S. Army, Vietnam, received a presidential plaque for its outstanding accomplishments in reducing costs and improving management in a combat environment. In addition to this award, the Army received presidential certificates for twenty individuals and one organization in recognition of contributions to improve management and efficiency in government.

Progress in the Resources Conservation Program continued during fiscal year 1971 when $638.2 million was saved against a goal of $346 million. The actions taken in fiscal year 1971 were estimated to have a three-year saving effect of $1,253 million. Several examples illustrate participation in the program.

DEPARTMENT OF THE ARMY
CHRONOLOGY OF THE FISCAL YEAR 1971 BUDGET
BUDGET AUTHORITY[a]

(In millions of dollars)

Program Element	DA Submission to OSD	President's Budget	Enacted	Supplemental Budget Enacted
Military personnel, Army	8,566.0	7,923.7	7,842.5	660.0
Reserve personnel, Army	341.3	336.5	334.8	25.9
National Guard personnel, Army	385.0	387.1	387.1	39.5
Operation and maintenance, Army	7,131.0	6,332.0	6,268.7	252.3
Operation and maintenance, Army National Guard	286.2	287.4	287.4	23.9
National Board for the Promotion of Rifle Practice		.1	.1	
Procurement of equipment and missiles, Army	4,458.0	3,226.0	2,908.5	
Research, development, test, and evaluation, Army	1,716.0	1,717.9	1,600.2	7.7
Subtotal excluding construction	(22,883.5)	(20,210.7)	(19,629.2)	(1,009.2)
Military Construction, Army	392.0	708.0	647.0	
Military Construction, Army Reserve	10.0	10.0	10.0	
Military Construction, Army National Guard	15.0	15.0	15.0	
Subtotal, construction accounts	(417.0)	(733.0)	(672.0)	
Total budget authority	23,300.5	20,943.7	20,301.1	1,009.2

[a]Figures may not add due to rounding.

DEPARTMENT OF THE ARMY
BUDGET OUTLAYS, FISCAL YEARS 1969, 1970, 1971

(In thousands of dollars)

	Fiscal Year 1969	Fiscal Year 1970	Fiscal Year 1971
Military personnel, Army	8,460,678	9,017,713	8,605,186
Reserve personnel, Army	270,796	303,531	353,285
National Guard personnel, Army	315,913	379,718	440,445
Operation and maintenance, Army . .	8,029,939	7,570,197	7,186,626
Operation and maintenance, ARNG . .	269,734	308,913	318,488
National Board for the Promotion of Rifle Practice	38	41	68
Procurement of equipment and missiles, Army	6,116,741	5,206,121	4,359,685
Research, development, test, and evaluation, Army	1,520,840	1,665,477	1,568,753
Military Construction, Army	450,324	438,908	483,970
Military Construction, AR	1,508	7,993	4,853
Military Construction, ARNG	8,377	10,993	13,178
Defense production guarantee.	−20	−22	1
Army Stock Fund	−305,119	−131,183	−148,966
Army Industrial Fund	−34,958	12,713	−20,717
Army Management Fund	−7,802	5,178	4,447
Subtotal	25,096,989	24,796,291	23,169,302
Army Trust Fund	82	108	252
Trust revolving funds	2,042	−732	−2,790
Miscellaneous receipts	−63,864	−46,592	−45,014
Total budget outlays	25,035,249	24,749,075	23,121,750

Fin and nozzle assemblies for the 2.75 rocket motor were procured as complete assemblies. A study was made to determine the possible advantages of purchasing complete assemblies as compared with purchasing fin blades separately and furnishing them to contractors for inclusion in the total assembly. As a result of this study, fin blades are now purchased separately, with resultant savings of $230,700.

By using a newly developed loading technique which increases the carrying capacity of the C-141 aircraft from two helicopters to three, the Army saved $732,000 in air shipment costs to Vietnam in the first eight months of fiscal year 1971.

Cost Analysis and Audits

The U.S. Army Field Operating Cost Agency conducted a data-collection trip in Germany, Korea, and the continental United States during the fiscal year. Direct operating costs were computed for the 2d and 7th Infantry Divisions and for selected I Corps units in Korea. As the year closed a unit readiness reporting cost model was nearing completion which should provide Army planners with a tool for determining force unit readiness level costs. In addition, direct operating costs were being developed for all active Army divisions.

The agency also collected and analyzed field data from Korea, Germany, and Vietnam. Emphasis was placed on aircraft operating costs. The costs per flying hour were developed by geographical area for fixed- and rotary-wing aircraft.

In Vietnam, operation and maintenance cost factors were developed based on U.S. and Vietnamese Regional and Popular Forces combat strength. A comparison was made of the costs of a Vietnamese Army and U.S. Army division slice.

During the fiscal year the U.S. Army Audit Agency assumed responsibility for auditing 75 percent of the officer and noncommissioned officer open messes and clubs. Initial audits were to be completed by June 1972, with annual audits to follow. Since audits of open messes differ from normal mission-type audits, it was necessary to develop new audit techniques, to expand auditor training, and to perfect audit guides. By midyear these requirements had been met, an addition to the audit manual had been published, and a firm schedule of open mess audits had been undertaken. In April 1971, a bulletin on lessons learned from early audits was issued to major commanders Army-wide. By the end of the fiscal year the Army Audit Agency was on schedule for the initial audits of Army open messes, lessons learned were being applied by commanders, and the internal controls over open mess operations were being significantly strengthened.

IX. Logistics

Logistics as it is known today is the science of planning and carrying out the movement and maintenance of forces. A century or more ago, logistics might have been described as getting there first with the most. In today's more sophisticated and more carefully managed environment, it means getting there with the right amount of support when needed. In other words, it means providing the American soldier with what he needs, where and when he needs it, and in the condition and quantity required for his use, all within the framework of available monetary resources.

The Army's logistics mission in fiscal year 1971 has been to support combat operations in a limited war; support allies as they replace U.S. combat forces; maintain a high state of combat readiness for both U.S. and allied forces; and maintain a modern and responsive industrial base. This chapter describes the highlights of operations related to procurement, maintenance, supply, transportation, facilities, construction, military assistance, and support services.

The economic benefits of the Logistics Offensive Program continued to grow at a rapid rate. At the close of the fiscal year, the total amounted to approximately $6.1 billion. Of this amount, $4.5 billion has a direct impact on the Army's budget requirements. While the balance of these benefits is not related directly to the budget, it represents bonus effects from such things as reduced training requirements, increased efficiency, and improved readiness.

Materiel Acquisition

In fiscal year 1971, $3.6 billion was allocated for equipment, missile, and ammunition procurement, about a billion dollars less than 1970. The program was designed to provide prudent stock levels in the light of the diminishing commitment in Southeast Asia. Over $1.2 billion involved war-related procurement as compared with $4.5 billion in 1969. The table compares costs in the various commodity categories over the past three years.

Of the $5.1 billion in contracts awarded during the year, $4.2 billion ($3 billion from current year and $1.2 billion from prior-year funds) was for the Army and $900 million for customers who buy Army equipment and ammunition.

Ammunition procurement programs for fiscal years 1969–1971

ARMY PROCUREMENT PROGRAM

(In millions of dollars)

	1969	Fiscal Year 1970	1971
Aircraft	570.0	341.8	206.0
Aircraft spares and repair parts	130.5	74.5	14.0
Missiles	868.6	770.4	935.9
Missile spares and repair parts	38.9	37.6	20.2
(Safeguard system)	(330.6)	(360.5)	(651.0)
Weapons and combat vehicles	485.6	275.6	286.7
Tactical and support vehicles	391.9	435.7	395.4
Communications and electronics equipment	533.4	320.8	200.9
Other support equipment	407.8	254.8	118.5
Ammunition	2,766.3	1,731.2	1,146.6
Production base support	148.9	342.9	237.2
Total	6,341.9	4,585.3	3,561.4

were developed to meet fixed requirements; contingency procurement was excluded because an active production base was operating in case of need, and balance could be maintained between allocations and requirements by drawing upon depot stocks and extending procurement schedules. Although consumption rates varied significantly during the period, no critical shortages occurred.

As the Army must have its equipment readily available to respond to emergencies, it owns certain manufacturing facilities and industrial equipment to produce a significant portion of its materiel, particularly ammunition. This production base, most of it still active, is valued at nearly $9 billion. The Army also owns approximately $400 million in tools used by contractors in private plants.

This production base was constructed in great part during the early days of World War II. Wartime exigencies made it virtually impossible to develop new production techniques or, in some cases, to wait until more desirable construction materials became available. Although these plants, which were used during the Korean and Vietnam Wars, were idle during peacetime, funds were available for minimum maintenance only, not for rehabilitation and modernization. Thus today many of these facilities are outdated, present safety hazards, and raise pollution problems.

The Army is in the third year of a program to modernize ammunition production facilities. At current budgetary levels the Army will need from eighteen to twenty years to complete the $3 billion program. Priority is being given to eliminating hazards connected with the production of explosives and propellants. Pollution is also receiving attention in line with executive orders.

Materiel Maintenance

Under the Maintenance Support Positive program, there was progress in fiscal year 1971 in tailoring maintenance concepts to specific commodity and weapons systems—part of the effort to achieve maximum materiel readiness at minimum cost. Systems were reviewed to determine where piece-part repair and modular replacement could be most effectively employed. Also, under the Army Maintenance Management System, evaluations were made of the need for maintenance operational records and requirements to report maintenance data to Department of the Army and Department of Defense levels. New data -collection techniques were developed so that record-keeping and reporting related to the maintenance of Army equipment was brought to a level appropriate to the resources required to manage it.

Fiscal year 1971 saw the continued application of certain projects designed to reduce the number of repair parts selected and shipped with equipment as initial support items. Concepts were developed in 1969 and guidance issued to insure that only the required range and quantities of repair parts would be designated for initial distribution; and while the 1971 experience had not produced sufficient data for firm estimates, by year's end a reduction of 25 to 30 percent in repair parts initially furnished the soldier seemed likely.

Also promulgated during the year were standards for the maintenance, care, and preservation of prepositioned equipment, which is not covered by existing guidance concerning materiel used by the active Army and in the depot system. Maintenance standards for prepositioned materiel are essential to insure that it is ready for use under emergency conditions.

Management of the distribution of selected items throughout the Army's supply and maintenance systems under the so-called Closed Loop Support Program was expanded to cover additional commands and items, while a new "Call Forward" procedure was initiated in United States Army, Pacific, to safeguard against over-stockage in a period of rapidly changing requirements.

Recent studies have concluded that about 75 percent of the Army's tire replacement requirements can be satisfied by using retread tires. Maximum use of retreads has become Army policy, and indeed the Army has been assigned a leading role in the Department of Defense tire management program. During fiscal year 1971, over 302,000 tires were retreaded, resulting in savings of $9.9 million.

Depot materiel maintenance and support funding totaled about $668.8 million in direct obligations in fiscal year 1971, including $515.8 million for depot maintenance activities, $10.2 million for base operations costs, $6.5 million for technical, administrative, and new equipment training, and $136.3 million for maintenance support activities.

Although inspections are recognized as necessary tools in any effective management program, they can be both expensive and burdensome if they are not properly conducted. Thus in fiscal year 1971 the Army challenged both the concept and the objectives of command maintenance management inspection (CMMI) to determine the extent of harassment and irritation caused by unannounced inspections and the costs associated with preparations for team visits. Under the Maintenance Assistance and Instruction Team (MAIT) program, procedures were modified to reduce both irritants and costs by eliminating unannounced inspections, preparations for inspection, and scoring of units, and by using personnel resources at the post-division level for MAIT rather than at the Army command level to support the CMMI's.

Aviation Logistics

Because logistic support requirements for Army-type aircraft used by U.S. and allied forces in Southeast Asia were substantially enlarged with the transfer to Vietnamese forces of a large number of helicopters under the Vietnamization program, a single pipeline was established to support these forces. The consolidation of the pipeline for aircraft components and repair parts increased aircraft availability and reduced costs. Goals were set, under the over-all program, to reduce the aviation repair parts and components in U.S. Army, Vietnam. Pipeline control over aircraft engines has made it possible to reduce procurement and release existing stocks for installation in new aircraft. As the fiscal year closed, details were being worked out for a single Army repair parts and components pipeline to support all Army aircraft in the Far East, including those used by allied as well as U.S. armed forces.

Attention was also focused during the year on using the heavy lift helicopter (HLH) in the Army's worldwide logistics mission. A study project (Log Lift) addressed all facets of the HLH role to determine its cost and effectiveness in comparison with other modes of transportation and to develop estimates as to the quantity required.

Supply and Depot Management

The Department of the Army Distribution-Allocation Committee was established to provide Department of the Army staff control over allocations of critical items of supply during the buildup of Army forces in Vietnam. During fiscal year 1971 the committee's emphasis shifted from expediting logistical support to Southeast Asia to preventing the buildup of excess stocks as redeployment modified requirements. More attention was given to Continental Army Command and Reserve Component readiness, and these units were provided M16 rifles, tactical and combat vehicles, trailers, radios, and engineer equipment, all made available as a result of the diminishing commitment in Southeast Asia.

At the same time, modernization actions were implemented in U.S. Army, Europe.

The Army Stock Fund finances much of the materiel that flows through the depot system. Stock Fund purchase authority in fiscal year 1971 amounted to $2.6 billion, about 12 percent under 1970, while the issue program was $3.1 billion, about 14 percent below the previous year. Changes in stockage requirements and continuing decline in demands reduced stockage levels at all echelons of supply. A test of a direct delivery support system was made to some of the units in oversea commands. This system has further reduced oversea operating stockage requirements. Test results will be analyzed in the first quarter of fiscal year 1972. If the increased cost at the wholesale level of providing direct support can be offset by significant savings in inventory levels without degrading unit readiness, direct delivery will be extended to other areas.

Modernization of depot storage facilities in the United States began in fiscal year 1967 as part of a $14.7 million three-year program to equip the depots with the most efficient materiel-handling systems and in general to modernize facilities. By the end of fiscal year 1971 the original program had been completed with an expenditure of $12.4 million for handling equipment and alterations to facilities and $2.3 million for military construction. As a result of this modernization, 294 personnel spaces representing $1.98 million in annual operating costs had been saved through fiscal year 1971. When the program is completed in December 1972, 524 spaces and $3.9 million in depot operating costs will have been saved.

There were refinements during the year in the distribution management of petroleum products, which concerns Army units throughout the world. Terminal reporting was standardized for all services, and all regulations pertaining to petroleum management were consolidated into one regulation. Computations related to reserve requirements were also refined with the publication of a revised bulletin. The relationship between civilian and military distribution systems was strengthened.

Transportation

In fiscal year 1971 there was a decline in the movement of cargo and passengers worldwide. A total of 12,681,500 measurement tons of Army-sponsored cargo was moved over-ocean by the Military Sealift Command, 2,687,900 tons less than in fiscal year 1970. In addition, 189,900 short tons were airlifted by the Military Airlift Command. This was 37,100 tons less than in fiscal year 1970.

The policy of using airlift for the over-ocean movement of passengers as the most expeditious means with resulting savings in man-days of travel was continued in fiscal year 1971. A total of 1,208,000 Army sponsored passengers were moved by the Military Airlift Command, 365,400 less than the number airlifted in fiscal year 1970. Movement of passengers over-ocean by surface amounted to 88,100, about 11,800 lower than in fiscal year 1970.

A curb on the use of premium transportation was maintained through the year under the Airlift Challenge Program, which provides for automatic review, screening, and challenge of requests from field commands. An average of 3,500 shipments per month was diverted from airlift to sealift at an estimated savings of about $8.5 million per month, all without detriment to delivery dates.

Military standard transportation and movement procedures (MIL-STAMP) continued to provide an effective standard program for worldwide movement and documentation of cargo within the Defense Transportation System. MILSTAMP was improved during the report period by expanding the provisions covering break-bulk and documentation of container shipments of ammunition, explosives, and other dangerous articles.

In the field of containerization, production proceeded during the year on a total procurement of 6,700 containers (called MILVAN's), with a completion date of October 1972. As the year closed there were 2,600 leased containers in the MILVAN pilot program, while there were 4,287 chassis on hand of the 5,600 on order. Military transportation managers are considering the use of MILVAN's for contingency deployments, their use by the Navy and Air Force, containerized ammunition distribution systems, and container use for general cargo service worldwide and in the direct delivery test program covered under support of operations in Europe.

The exploitation of surface containerization became Department of Defense policy during the fiscal year, and the Army established a project manager's office, staffed by all of the military services, to develop container-supported distribution systems for all services.

During fiscal year 1971, the Army initiated action to evaluate current and future Army rail capabilities and requirements. This evaluation will culminate in the establishment of policy, procedures, and responsibilities for the Army rail fleet. The Army's policy has been to maintain a diversified rail fleet with sufficient motive power and rolling stock to meet daily peacetime requirements for utility railroad operation on a post, camp, or station.

Logistics Improvements in Supply, Maintenance, and Transportation

A major challenge in the logistics field in fiscal year 1971 was to do the planning and take the actions that would insure the continuation of a strong and viable logistics base in the United States and an efficient and effective logistics system around the world in a period when combat operations, oversea deployment, and over-all strength were diminishing. Thus the Streamline program, a logistics operation described in last year's report as it was begun in the Army's Pacific and European commands, was extended in the 1971 fiscal year to the Continental Army Command, Army commands in Alaska and Panama, and the Reserve Components. The actions were administered selectively to meet the needs of individual cases.

In the Continental Army Command the concepts and plans for initiating the direct supply support system were developed while storage operations, property disposal, and distribution programs were reviewed and refined. In the Army's Southern Command, logistic support activities were consolidated, while in Alaska the entire logistic support system and organization was studied. The objectives and actions of the Streamline program in the Reserve Components were similar to those of the active Army.

As the fiscal year opened there were about 1.4 million items of supply with federal stock numbers in the Army's supply system. A concerted effort was begun to reduce this supply, by limiting Army requisitioners to items only in the active portion of the Army Master Data File (Army catalog); by reducing the number of catalog items, through elimination of slow-moving items and cutting-back on the great range of types, sizes, and grades of an item; and by reconciling field data banks with the master file to assure that all echelons in the supply system are current in base data and are using the same identification, units of issue, prices, and other management data. By the end of the year the Army catalog had been reduced to 1.2 million items.

Stockage policies for support activities of the Army in the field were modified during the year. The number of items to be stocked below the continental U.S. depot level were reduced from 1,063,000 federal stock numbers at the opening of fiscal year 1970 to 327,000 at the close of fiscal year 1971. Here again the aim is to reduce inventory investment by eliminating stockage of slow-moving items below depot level. Fewer items will improve management, while more economical ordering will reduce requisitions and transaction volume both in administration and handling.

Under Project Clean, review of supply stockage in Vietnam indicates that during fiscal year 1971 the levels were reduced by over $189 million. This reduction was the result of judicious control over supply requisitions for both U.S. and allied forces, of normal attrition, of redistribution within Vietnam, and of the withdrawal of stocks. Also during the year, some $525 million in excess stocks was disposed of through

sale, redistribution, or return to the United States. As the year closed
there was about $24 million of identified excess materiel on hand in Viet-
nam depots. Redistribution of excess materiel from the Pacific area
under the PURA program was expedited through an accelerated cycle that reduced screening time from 300 to 75 days. At the same time,
requisition and shipment control under Project Stop-See led to can-
cellations of some $650 million worth of materiel no longer needed in
Vietnam (including $136 million for fiscal year 1971). Under Proj-
ect Transplant, technical evaluation assistance teams, composed of
specialists in sales management and scrap processing, helped develop
procedures to expedite the removal of scrap from Vietnam, by dealing with off-shore test sales, property disposal priorities, and shipment
by military sea-lift of surplus materiel at special rates to selected Pacific
area ports.

The test of a direct support system for commissaries in Europe, described in last year's report and launched as that period was closing,
was applied to six stores. A midperiod evaluation in October 1970 indicated that the concept was feasible, and the test was extended to June
1971. The program will be expanded during fiscal year 1972 to include a total of thirty-five stores.

During fiscal year 1971 the initial phase was completed of an
automatic data processing system that provides a monthly record of
air and surface transportation movements in tons of passengers from
the continental United States to oversea destinations as well as from
overseas to the United States. The first phase of the system was designed
to eliminate the time-consuming manual manipulation of tonnage data,
which often took from forty-five to sixty days to formulate, and provide
more accurate data within fifteen days.

Logistics Doctrine and Systems

There were developments in a number of logistic systems during
the year. The Division Logistics System was expanded to include all
Seventh Army divisions, three in the Continental Army Command,
one in Eighth Army, and a brigade assigned to U.S. Army, Hawaii.
The system standardizes stock control management procedures by auto-
mating functional tasks. It improves the quality and flow of data, sim-
plifies procedures for soldiers with limited experience, and promotes
a smooth transition to future automated systems.

One of the techniques tested during the year to offset the impact of reductions in materiel procurement authorizations, operating funds, and personnel was the Direct Support System (DSS). This
system provides for a reduction of oversea depot stockage levels by
routing replenishment shipments direct from the continental United

States to direct support units in oversea areas. Under this practice, oversea depot stockage levels are limited to theater reserve and project materiel plus a safety level for items supported by theater demands and not included in reserve and project stocks.

The DSS uses two theater-oriented depot complexes—one on the east coast serving Europe, one on the west coast serving the Pacific— and a logistics control office in San Francisco. Each complex utilizes one of its depots as a consolidation point for the containerization or palletization of shipments, and the control office maintains a computerized logistic intelligence file to control all phases of the system.

Following an Army-wide review of the logistic system to validate current and developmental systems and achieve greater standardization in materiel support at the intermediate levels in the continental United States and overseas, a standard Army intermediate level system (SAILS) was approved; development of the system was in progress as the year closed. Also developed was a selected item management system that will provide management control over materiel with special characteristics of cost and need. Development continued on the Logistics Master Plan, which will guide the development and maintenance of the Standard Army Logistics System. Also, the Army Materiel Command continued to work on the five-year automatic data processing program intended to standardize its automated systems.

Facilities and Construction

The 1971 Military Construction Authorization Act approved on October 26, 1970, provided $264.9 million in new funding authorization for the Army, added to $325.2 million that had already been approved on October 7, 1970, under Public Law 91–441 for Safeguard construction. A fiscal year 1971 military construction appropriation of $646.9 million in new obligational authority was approved in December 1970.

The Army in fiscal year 1971 thus had available for military construction a total of $1,099.8 million: $647 million in current appropriations; $408.9 million in unobligated carry-over from prior-year appropriations; $12.6 million transferred from Department of Defense military construction contingency funds; and $31.3 million from recoupments in the infrastructure program. The funds for new work were allocated as follows:

	(in millions of dollars)
Major projects (excluding Vietnam, Thailand, and Safeguard)	413.6
Vietnam and Thailand	93.2
Safeguard (including planning, access roads, and community support)	452.7
Infrastructure	89.5
General authorization	50.8
Total	1,099.8

Delay in congressional action on the fiscal year 1970 appropriation bill limited construction starts during the first half to projects authorized and funded in prior years. Temporary delays in contract awards also resulted from the suspension of the Davis-Bacon Act provisions (prohibiting discrimination in hiring on government contract jobs) during the period February 23–March 29, 1971. A total of thirty-nine MCA (Military Construction, Army) projects valued at $88.2 million were awarded without Davis-Bacon Act provisions. Results of the suspension on contract costs were inconclusive. Inflationary pressure on construction costs continued during the year, limiting progress in reducing the backlog of unawarded projects.

Construction awards to improve and update industrial facilities at government-owned plants totaled about $53.5 million. During the year thirty-seven projects were completed at a cost of $16 million.

At the beginning of fiscal year 1971 there was $68.2 million in unobligated military construction funds for Southeast Asia, including $34.2 million in unapportioned funds for Vietnam from fiscal year 1969. Congress approved $25 million more in construction funds for Vietnam in 1971, and by the close of the fiscal year all had been apportioned, with the unobligated balance totaling $47.9 million. Over $1.3 billion in regular, supplemental, contingency, and military assistance funds were allocated to military construction in Southeast Asia during fiscal years 1965–1971.

Long-range, military construction, known requirements (exclusive of family housing, Safeguard, and NATO infrastructure) amount to $6.9 billion. Over $4 billion is required to eliminate the backlog of projects to replace temporary frame structures constructed in World War II and modernize permanent structures in line with current standards. Funds for these purposes are limited to $400 million annually.

The Army, through its Corps of Engineers, provided construction support to numerous agencies and projects, among them the Air Force (including its National Guard and Reserve); the National Aeronautics and Space Administration; the Department of Health, Education, and Welfare; the U.S. Postal Service; various Department of Defense agencies; the Agency for International Development; the U.S. Information Agency; the Trust Territory of the Pacific Islands; the Robert F. Kennedy gravesite; national cemeteries; and various foreign governments. During the fiscal year Army engineers contracted for approximately $457 million of construction for these purposes.

To establish a reserve of nontactical mobile electric power, high voltage generators that are excess to needs in Vietnam will be returned to the United States. A survey was conducted by the Army Corps of Engineers to identify recoverable generators and ancillary equipment for shipment to the zone of the interior during the next two fiscal years. This equipment, added to the four existing power barges, will provide the Army with about 170,000 kilowatts of generating capacity for use in contingency operations, natural disasters, and other emergencies.

The Army is one of the largest real estate agencies in the world, with broad responsibilities for base and installation planning, administration, construction, and operation. There were numerous actions in this general area during fiscal year 1971. Under Executive Order 11508 the Army reviewed its real property holdings to assess the degree of utilization. Commanders were directed to review all real property under their jurisdiction and to report excess holdings for disposal. A study of long-range stationing requirements was made to identify priorities for retention of installations under various projected force levels. An Army installations planning committee was established to review and make recommendations on the stationing of major units and activities, long-range strengths and missions for installations, military construction and family housing, and base development.

A number of changes regarding Army installations were announced during the year. Scheduled to be closed are the Burlington Army Ammunition Plant in New Jersey, the Gateway Army Ammunition Plant in Missouri, the Lawndale Army Missile Plant in California, the Sunflower Army Ammunition Plant in Kansas, and Fort Wadsworth in New York. The Burlington, Gateway, and Sunflower plants will be retained in a standby status. Also announced and accomplished during the year were the consolidation of base operations of the Aberdeen Proving Ground and Edgewood Arsenal in Maryland and the closure of Two Rock Ranch Station in California. Edgewood Arsenal was disestablished as an installation and concurrently established as a class II activity at Aberdeen Proving Ground. Two Rock Ranch Station was transferred to the Department of Transportation. The Coraopolis Army Tank–Automotive Steel Foundry in Pennsylvania and the Muskegon Army Engine Plant in Michigan were discontinued as Department of the Army installations.

An Army base development board was established in October 1970 to explore facility requirements, identify command and departmental staff responsibilities, and examine ways of improving base development planning and Army support of contingency operations. New regulations were published to assist commanders and staff officers in base development; a base development planning assistance office was established; and a computer-assisted system for engineer planning was developed. And development continued on an integrated facilities system to provide accurate and timely information on Army real property resources and programs.

Expenditures for real property maintenance activities at Army installations in fiscal year 1971 were slightly over $1 billion. Building space decreased by about 36 million square feet as some facilities were discontinued. Unfinanced real property maintenance and repair at the close of the fiscal year was approximately $368 million, a decrease of 4 percent from 1970.

Several major programs were in progress during the year, at home and overseas, to renovate or replace old and inadequate facilities. One was the design and construction of a new Walter Reed General Hospital. Another was the renovation of troop living facilities for U.S. Army personnel in Germany.

The background of the Walter Reed General Hospital project is of interest. Major William Clive Borden, commander of the hospital at Washington Barracks in the nation's capital, was the first to envision a complete medical center capable of carrying on research, teaching, and care of the sick and wounded. In 1905, Congress authorized construction of Walter Reed U.S. Army General Hospital, and in May 1909 the new eighty-bed hospital opened.

Many physical changes have taken place at Walter Reed in its short history. In 1967, initial planning began to replace the now inadequate facilities that constitute the general hospital at the Army's prime medical center. Thirty-five separately constructed, interconnected buildings (some dating back to 1909) will be replaced by a new 1,280-bed hospital.

A team of nationally recognized medical architects and special consultants was retained to design the new facility. Concept design was completed in June 1969. It provides for the most modern health care facilities and will be able to accommodate technical advances and will be assured of a more extended life span than has been possible heretofore with conventional design.

The new hospital, now in final design, will provide for thirty-seven medical specialties and will be the heart of a patient care, teaching, and research center. The new hospital is expected to provide not only the Army but the nation with a medical resource of unlimited human value.

In another stateside action, the United States Military Academy Planning Advisory Board was established. Composed of eleven members appointed by the Secretary of the Army from civilian life and the ranks of retired senior military officers, the board will review and make recommendations concerning the USMA construction program.

In Europe, essential programs concerned the renovation of troop living facilities in some 120 old German kasernes and the replacement of old coal-burning boilers with more reliable and economical oil-burning boilers in heating plants. In the light of fund limitations for the barrack renovation program, greater emphasis is being placed on selective rehabilitation to correct the worst living conditions, and on procurement of supplies to support the troop self-help program and the facilities engineer effort.

In December 1967 the Secretary of the Army was assigned responsibility for the Homeowners Assistance Program, under which military and civilian employees of the Department of Defense are provided financial assistance to reduce their losses if they are required to dispose of a home when a military installation is closed or activities are curtailed. Through June 30, 1971, 9,351 applications for assistance had been received and 5,581 applicants had been given assistance totaling $15.024 million. Some 1,316 mortgages totaling $10.751 million were assumed, while 2,075 applications were rejected.

Support of Operations in Europe

The logistics posture and combat effectiveness of U.S. Army, Europe, improved during the year as a result of the introduction of new equipment and the modernization of existing materiel. Newly developed armored reconnaissance vehicles were supplied to armored cavalry squadrons; helicopters were modernized; Pershing equipment was converted from tracks to wheels and the Hawk to a self-propelled configuration; and air defense control centers and base defense were modernized. There were also improvements in the materiel readiness of units, in the status of war reserve stocks, and in protective construction. New communications equipment was issued and old equipment rebuilt, while Autovon facilities were extended throughout the command.

As noted earlier, a direct support system was tested during the year, designed to maintain and improve supply responsiveness with a reduced expenditure of resources by taking advantage of technological advances in communications, automated data processing, and transportation. The test was being carried out with a number of divisional and nondivisional direct and general support units in Europe and Korea as the year closed. An evaluation of the system is scheduled during September 1971.

Combat readiness in Europe was also furthered during the year in continuing preparations to house and maintain equipment for reinforcing units in case of need. Under this concept, deploying reinforcements would be issued prepositioned equipment on arrival in Europe from controlled humidity warehouses. The program to house this equipment was approximately 50 percent complete by the close of the fiscal year.

Actions to establish a wartime line of communications to provide emergency support for U.S. forces in central Europe, necessitated by the withdrawal from France, continued during 1971.

Under the military construction program, the Army continued to fund the U.S. share of the NATO Common Infrastructure Program. The Congress authorized $41.5 million and appropriated $33.5 million of the budget request. The other NATO nations continued their agreement to share the cost of relocating U.S. facilities from France. At the end of calendar year 1970, $28 million had been recouped. The remainder of relocation costs, up to the agreed-upon ceiling of $96 million, will be direct-funded by NATO at the rate of $5.6 million per quarter.

Military Assistance

The materiel portion of the 1971 Army Military Assistance Program (MAP), Grant Aid, totaled $729 million and included varying degrees of support for countries and international organizations. Grant aid recipients received $299 million in materiel, for which the Army was reimbursed, and $270 million without reimbursement during the fiscal year. Materiel delivered was predominantly from prior-year undelivered balances or from excess Army stocks.

Aid to Thailand and Laos, funded under military assistance service procedures, required special attention as a result of the war in Vietnam. Materiel orders amounting to $95 million were received from those countries and $78-million worth was delivered.

During the fiscal year the Army transferred, under special long supply and excess programs, materiel included above with an acquisition value of $190 million to MAP at no cost and an additional $4 million to Thailand and Laos. This program encourages participants to accept major items of excess materiel "as-is" with rehabilitation and shipping expenses being borne by the recipient. The Republic of China, Korea, Greece, and Turkey were the principal recipients of materiel under this program.

Through a combination grant aid and foreign military sales agreement, equipment for an additional air defense (Nike) unit was supplied to the Republic of China during the fiscal year. A large portion of this materiel was made available from Army excesses under the program described above, requiring no reimbursement from MAP funds. A program to modernize and improve Republic of Korea forces during the period 1971–1975 was begun in January 1971. Requirements are being filled by transfer of equipment from withdrawing U.S. units, from new procurement, and from Army long and excess supply. The cost will total $1.25 billion in funded increments and $0.25 billion from the long supply and excess program.

Cambodia received modest Army grant aid assistance amounting to $6.6 million in fiscal year 1970, increased to about $149 million in 1971.

The Strategic Communications Command continued to manage

and install fixed communications projects for allied countries during the year, including Spain, the Philippines, Thailand, Indonesia, and Iran.

Also during the year the Office of the Secretary of Defense directed the Department of the Army to supply selected quantities of grant aid materiel to Jordan with an estimated value of $21.5 million, the first such aid since 1967. A new MAP program was also initiated for Lebanon, the first since 1963.

Under a new base rights agreement with Spain, signed on August 6, 1970, and extending U.S. government use of Spanish bases to September 1975, the United States agreed to provide Spain through grant aid with specific quantities of helicopters, tanks, howitzers, guns, and various types of carriers, along with credit to purchase aircraft and a territorial communications command network.

The April 1967 suspension on delivery of selected military equipment to Greece was lifted in September 1970 and shipments were resumed.

In fiscal year 1971 the Army sold materiel and services valued at $540.6 million to fifty-eight countries and five international organizations. In conducting its sales activities the Army adhered to the policy that materiel readily available through commercial sources would be sold by U.S. industry directly to the recipient.

Under the Army's Logistical Orientation Tour Program a number of groups of high-ranking military personnel visited the United States to see new military systems and equipment of mutual interest in free world defense. Several demonstrations were conducted in Europe and the Far East.

The Army also participated in seventeen coproduction programs with six foreign nations and NATO, under which the foreign nations assemble or manufacture major end items or weapon systems of U.S. origin. These programs were valued at $1,502.3 million, with expenditures for goods and services in the United States valued at $559.3 million. Participating countries are the Republic of China, the Netherlands, Norway, Italy, the Federal Republic of Germany, and Japan. Items of U.S. origin being coproduced include the UH–1D and UH–1H helicopters, the M–60 tank, the M–113 armored personnel carrier family of vehicles, the M109 self-propelled howitzer, wheeled vehicles, a light antitank weapon, and small arms.

In the field of co-operative logistics, the Army maintained supply support arrangements with seventeen allied and friendly nations and with NATO. These programs provide participating countries with continuous follow-on support for major end items and weapon systems on a reimbursable basis. The program was valued at $173 million during the fiscal year and involved the support of a variety of items such as conventional weapons and vehicles and the Sergeant, Pershing, and Hawk missile systems.

International logistics management activity was broadened during the year to place increased emphasis on planning and provisioning for current and near year requirements. As U.S. Army procurements were reduced or acquisition objectives were satisfied, it became necessary to seek total 1971 fiscal year funding and some advance 1972 funding for international logistics customer requirements. This action was taken to combine procurement and take advantage of contract options. Major item groups were reviewed for possible procurement of equipment peculiar to international logistics program customers. When an item can no longer be provided economically by the U.S. Army supply system, it will be withdrawn; U.S. industry will provide direct support to countries on commercial items.

Support Services

The Army continued to administer eighty-five national cemeteries during the fiscal year. The proposal that the National Cemetery System be transferred to the Veterans Administration was kept before the Congress but not acted upon. There were 37,270 interments in the cemeteries in the 1971 period, 721 of them combat casualties interred in fifty-seven national cemeteries. Forty-six cemeteries were open for general interment, while thirty-nine were closed, with gravesites available only for combat casualties, pre-1962 reservations, and surviving family members. The Andersonville National Cemetery in Georgia was transferred to the Department of the Interior, the changeover to be effective July 1, 1971.

A total of 8,280 bodies of military, dependent, and civilian personnel on a worldwide basis were processed under the Army Mortuary Program during fiscal year 1971. Included in the total were twenty-four World War II casualties that were identified in Germany, the Netherlands, Okinawa, Celebes, and New Guinea. In addition, four other recoveries in New Guinea and Austria were being investigated.

The Subsistence Operations Review Board was formed in fiscal year 1971 to examine the Army Food Program, including all aspects of subsistence management, and with the broad mission of determining what actions in this area would contribute to recruitment and retention in the light of plans for an all-volunteer Army. The board visited Army units, industrial and educational facilities, food service installations, and the British Catering Corps as part of a study completed as the year closed. Recommendations will be considered for implementation in the coming year.

Over the past several years the military services have been gradually converting their food service programs from military to civilian staffs. Kitchen police (KP) duty was indentified in volunteer Army studies as one of the most unpopular tasks. The Army Staff developed a five-year program of civilianization that would ultimately require 23,400 spaces at an annual cost of $115 million.

Along another line, the Army proceeded with plans to test a contract food service operation in the metropolitan Washington area. The purpose is to determine the feasibility of using a civilian food service firm to provide the food, management, and personnel for military dining facilities. A one-year contract for $931,200 was awarded for this service at the Tri-Service Dining Facility, Fort Myer, Virginia.

In January 1971 the master menu was revised to include a daily short order menu. It provides for such popular items as hamburgers, cheeseburgers, frankfurters, and sandwiches, as well as french fried potatoes and potato chips. Soft drinks were also authorized for issue in Army dining facilities. The short order menu is served in addition to the regular dinner meal.

The Army commissary system also came in for some attention during the year with the preparation of a marketing guide to assist commissary officers in selecting stock to meet the needs and desires of their customers. With the guide, scheduled for publication in fiscal year 1972, customer satisfaction is expected to be enhanced while savings will accrue through less markdown and spoilage of goods.

During the period covered by this report, excess, surplus, and foreign excess personal property with an acquisition cost of $1.3 billion was turned over to Army property disposal activities for disposition by redistribution, transfer, donation, sale, or other authorized action. Useable property valued at $478.7 million and 511.8 thousand short tons of scrap were sold. The proceeds from sales amounted to $57.3 million, against a cost of $54.7 million for the disposal program.

Inventories of useable property for disposal decreased during the year from $564 million to $446 million.

X. Research and Development

Research is the continuing effort to acquire knowledge of natural phenomena and environment in order to solve problems in all fields of science. Development is the continuing application of the findings to create products and techniques for military purposes.

Budget

The fiscal year 1971 research, development, test, and evaluation (RDTE) budget as submitted to the Congress in January 1970 requested new obligation authority of $1,717.9 million and requested reauthorization of $18 million of prior-year funds for a total of $1,735.9 million. Public Law 91–441 authorized $1,635.6 million to be appropriated for fiscal year 1971. The lower figure was the result of specific reductions that included the $18-million reauthorization figure. The Department of Defense Appropriation Act of 1971 (Public Law 91–668), enacted on January 11, 1971, allocated $1,600.2 million for RDTE, to be used as authorized by law and to remain available for obligation until June 30, 1972. The fiscal year 1971 RDTE column of the fiscal year 1972 budget, as amended, came to a total of $1,612.075 and included adjustments for such things as transfers (minus $42.1 million), reprograming of prior-year funds (plus $5.2 million), and a proposed supplement for pay raises (plus $30.8 million).

The Army requested $1,841.6 million for the fiscal year 1972 RDTE program in a budget submitted on October 1, 1970. Following minor revisions and the addition of $117.7 million to finance new initiatives, the 1972 budget was submitted to Congress in January 1971 at a level of $1,932.1 million. In April 1971 another $17.9 million was added to provide for annual pay raises, effective in January 1971. The revised 1972 budget totaled $1,949.9 million.

A major change in the RDTE appropriation was issued as a part of the 1971 Department of Defense Appropriation Act (Public Law 91–668), stating that appropriations theretofore available under the RDTE categories could not be obligated after June 30, 1972; thus all unobligated balances would be lost to the Army. A language change in the 1972 budget authorized the appropriation to remain available until expended.

As a result of this situation, prior-year unobligated balances were reviewed and obligation and commitments carefully validated. Excess funds were to be returned to the central research and development bank to finance unscheduled high priority programs. Over $30 million was recouped during fiscal year 1971.

Maintaining a Technology Base

The technology base may be defined as the totality of means by which the Army develops the materiel, concepts, and techniques necessary to meet its current and future missions and roles. The base consists of an accumulation of scientific and technical knowledge, trained and experienced personnel, a responsive educational system, modern research and development facilities, and relevant research and development programs. These national resources, both internal and external, enable the Army to maintain superiority and avoid technological surprises from a potential enemy.

The fundamental reason why the Army needs to maintain a technology base stems from assigned missions, functions, and responsibilities. To remain a first-class fighting force, the Army must have better weapons, mobility, communications, medical treatment, and other military essentials. To fulfill these needs, the Army must draw upon available science and technology and must also create new science and technology. These needs require that a vigorous basic and applied research program be conducted.

In addition to the fundamental reason for Army involvement in research and development, there are two "real world" situations that demand continued and even increased involvement. These inescapable facts are that the Army is getting smaller and the United States is in a period of strategic nuclear parity.

One of the ways in which the Army can add to its power, even while its size is diminishing, is with modern equipment—the hardware needed to maintain constant levels of effectiveness in such functions as firepower, mobility, and communications. Research and exploratory development are at the very heart of new product development and old product improvement. The Army has been, and will continue to be, one of the largest consumers of technology in the country. It must, therefore, be an intelligent buyer of technology. To be an intelligent buyer, the Army must be technically competent. To be technically competent, it must do in-house work, including basic research.

The ultimate goal of total Army involvement in research and exploratory development is to improve, through knowledge, the effectiveness of its operational forces. In order to achieve this goal, the Army must ensure that all technological areas important to the Army are exploited. Some of the areas that are of particular concern to the Army, or in which it has a dominant role, are explosives, ground mobility, and tropical medicine. The Army must be the leader and actually perform the bulk of the research in these areas, or the work would simply not be done.

The Army must also engage in many other areas of research that are covered by other organizations in the federal government, in industry, and in the academic world. A few examples are electronics, materials, and meterology. Active participation by the Army in such areas assures that the results of research, wherever done, are applied to Army problems and that specific problem areas, unique to the Army, are addressed by Army laboratories.

Under nuclear parity, maintenance of adequate conventional forces becomes increasingly vital. These conventional forces are concentrated in the Army. They could be called general purpose forces, prepared to fight general purpose wars. These forces must be modern in order to make more efficient use of the manpower available in a smaller army. The Army must rely on research and exploratory development to provide the qualitative superiority in hardware necessary in light of U.S. force level reductions. As research efforts create new technologies, the Army measures them against priority requirements and then fully supports and funds the appropriate technological advances that will provide necessary capabilities.

The age of nuclear parity has, in part, been the result of increased emphasis, on the part of the Soviet Union, in research and development. According to Dr. John S. Foster, the Director of Defense Research and Engineering, who addressed the Navy League members in Miami, Florida, on December 5, 1970, "The Soviets now seem to be gaining on the United States in some areas of technology at a rate of about one year in every three or four. If present trends continue, the USSR could assume technological superiority in military research and development in the latter half of this decade." In other words, "The present relative trends in quality—research and development—coupled with comparable trends in quantity—development of numbers of improved weapons—could jeopardize the U.S. margin of security by the late 70's or early 80's." The loss of U.S. technological superiority would markedly reduce U.S. understanding of the intelligence that is collected, and consequently would seriously reduce the confidence we would have in making decisions about future weapons systems. Recovery from any loss of U.S. technological leadership would not be feasible without enormous expenditures over many years—and without a grave risk, meanwhile, of losing the national margin of safety.

This is a time of great adjustment for the Army. The drastic force reductions are not easy to manage. The Vietnamization of the war is a tremendous challenge. The Army's mission of providing national security, with diminishing resources in the face of a more powerful threat, is a difficult one. A vigorous research and exploratory program —properly managed—is an invaluable asset in assisting the Army to emerge from this transition period with a newer, smaller, tougher, higher quality force—an Army that will continue to meet the demands that are made of it.

Research and Development Programs

Under the impetus of a large-scale guerrilla-type war in Southeast Asia, important advances have been made in U.S. find-the-enemy capability—the result of increased emphasis in the fields of surveillance, target acquisition, and night observation (STANO). In July 1969, a management structure was established—including a system manager initially assigned in the Office of the Chief of Staff and now assigned to the Office of the Assistant Chief of Staff for Force Developments— to give direction, control, and emphasis in this special field. A STANO division was established in the Office of the Chief of Research and Development to supervise the evolution of techniques and hardware relating to night vision, radar, sensors, and special purpose detectors.

Attention continued at a high level in fiscal year 1971, and progress was made along all lines. Models of a French-German radar were procured to be sent to Vietnam for testing, and this system was placed in the normal development cycle. Engineering development continued on the AN/PPS–15 short-range company-level surveillance radar.

In the night vision area, technology was advanced through exploitation of the techniques of image intensification and thermal imagery. Comparative testing of various aerial night vision systems was completed by the MASSTER (Modern Army Selected Systems Test, Evaluation, and Review) test facility at Fort Hood, Texas. In these tests, FAAR infrared systems performed particularly well and are considered to have high potential for the future.

Experience with unattended ground sensors continued to indicate their potential for surveillance and target acquisition. In fiscal year 1971 a plan for the remotely monitored battlefield sensor system (REMBASS) program was approved, funds were allocated, and guidance was provided to the development agency. Under the program, unattended ground sensor technology will be adapted to a variety of applications.

More work is required to achieve an acceptable mix of capabilities. The ability to locate hostile weapons will receive increased attention in the coming year. Previous work in weapons-locating radar will permit a start on engineering development for the countermortar radar program and advanced development for the counterbattery radar program.

STANO technology, coupled with advances in automatic data processing and communications, portends an integrated battlefield control system that will materially assist the tactical commander in making sound and timely decisions.

During fiscal year 1971 the development programs of the mechanized infantry combat vehicle (MICV) and the armored reconnaissance scout vehicle (ARSV) were reoriented to some degree. In the fall of 1970 the ARSV program was modified to place it on an austere footing. In the early months of 1971 the mechanized infantry combat vehicle program development goals were broadened and both the MICV and ARSV programs were directed along austere lines with the MICV receiving the first priority in the event that future fiscal constraints require a priority determination to be made.

The Army's main battle tank, designated the MBT–70 under the former joint development program with the Federal Republic of Germany and redesignated the XM–803 under the U.S. unilateral continuation program, progressed during the year through design review and to definition of the revised configuration. Fabrication of advanced production engineering pilot tanks proceeded. These tanks will be used for engineering and expanded service tests. First production is scheduled for December 1975. Despite the major changes in the program, the production schedules set under the previous co-operative effort remained in phase.

With respect to the XM–803 engine, a source of concern to congressional committees, the United States returned to the air-cooled piston engine that had been dropped in favor of the German liquid-cooled engine. The reversion was made after study by military panels and after a detailed review by independent experts. The conclusion was that the U.S. engine, with a more conservative power rating, would be reliable and would be within the reasonable limits of development risks. At its new rating—1250 versus the 1475 horsepower of the earlier version—the engine will meet all user requirements. It represents, in comparison with any existing production engine in its class, an unprecedented engineering accomplishment in terms of both power per cubic foot and power per pound. Tests were highly encouraging and confirm its selection.

In the missile field, deployment of the TOW antitank system to the training base in the continental United States was essentially completed during the year. This tube-launched weapon is optically tracked and wire guided and is designed to be used by infantry and helicopter forces to destroy enemy tanks and other armored vehicles. It will replace the 106-mm. recoilless rifle and will improve the ability of U.S. forces to counter the armor threat that has existed in Europe since World War II.

Development of the Dragon system also advanced during the year. This weapon is light enough to be carried by one man and gives the foot soldier a lethal capability against enemy armor. It will replace the 90-mm. recoilless rifle, providing increased range, portability, and kill probability.

Surface-to-air-missile advanced development proceeded through the SAM–D system, the replacement for the Nike-Hercules and Hawk. Fabrication of the fire control group was completed and testing begun as component verification was continued. Captive flight tests were held to prove the guidance concept. Four propulsion test vehicles were flown, verifying the propulsion system and airframe in a limited flight environment. No fundamental technical problems were uncovered.

Under the Advanced Ballistic Missile Defense Program, the Advanced Ballistic Missile Defense Agency (ABMDA) continued work on new system concepts and components that led to improved defense capabilities. During the year a concept was formulated for the Hardsite defense system, intended to protect the Minuteman force against possible Soviet deployment of a larger and more sophisticated threat than that for which Safeguard is designed. Work continued also on a program to insure that data processing hardware and software techniques are capable of keeping pace with ballistic missile defense requirements; this program advances promising computer concepts not developed commercially, and also examines commercial computers for their adaptability to this role.

ABMDA also continued work on the concept of a long-range homing interceptor to engage and destroy hostile re-entry vehicles in midcourse, away from the continental United States. Development continued on an advanced terminal interceptor missile that would have the high velocity and maneuverability to counter the postulated future threats to the Minuteman force. Also being investigated was the feasibility of a homing capability for endoatmospheric interceptors.

Solid state radar and associated software work also proceeded; the small size, low power, and high reliability inherent in solid state devices will be exploited to reduce the investment, operating, and maintenance costs in future radar components.

An important part of the Advanced Ballistic Missile Defense Program is the identification, evaluation, and comparison of new system concepts that would provide paths for future development. Near term concepts build on Safeguard, while longer range ones depend upon more advanced technology.

In addition to the program described above, the ABMDA engages in a wide range of advanced technology projects. Current fields of investigation include radar, optics, missile and data processing components, nuclear vulnerability and lethality, system evaluation models, environmental measurements and experiments, and advanced materials and structures.

There were also a number of helicopter actions during the year. The period was devoted, for example, to the preparation and processing of documentation and plans for a program to develop a utility tactical transport aircraft system (UTTAS), the Army's first true squad carrier, to replace the UH–1 in assault helicopter companies, air cavalry units, and aeromedical evacuation units. Comparisons were made, in a cost effectiveness study, between proposed and existing candidate aircraft and in the light of a requirement for a helicopter capable of carrying an infantry squad.

In October 1970, funds were released for a joint Army-Navy heavy lift helicopter (HLH) program. Proposals from industry were evaluated and Boeing Vertol was selected on May 7, 1971, to design, fabricate, test, and demonstrate the critical components of an HLH capable of lifting a payload of 22.5 tons at sea level and at 95 degrees Fahrenheit.

The research and development program for an advanced aerial fire support system also continued during the year. A prototype AH–56A Cheyenne equipped with an improved rotor control system was flown at better than 200 knots true airspeed at design gross weight, and previous instabilities were overcome. Fabrication and ground test of the night vision system was completed and installation on an AH–56A initiated. Flight testing should follow in the coming fiscal year. Meanwhile, aerial firings of the TOW missile system were successfully conducted by Army gunners, with promising results for the Cheyenne system. Army pilots began testing the AH–56A helicopter in January 1971 and about 120 hours had been logged by the fiscal year's end.

Attention was also given during the year to aircraft electronics warfare self-protection equipment. Equipment, devices, and techniques being developed cover the entire range of electromagnetically controlled air defense weapons. Both passive and active devices to counter optical radar and infrared-controlled weapons are being investigated.

Finally, the Army also continued development work to improve conventional munitions, with considerable progress and promise in the use of submissiles and the techniques of controlled fragmentation.

XI. Civil Works and Military Engineering

The Army, through the Corps of Engineers civil works program, has been the principal developer of the nation's water resources. Recent years have seen a change in public policy toward all resource development, with the recognition that this nation's natural resources are finite. Yet a growing population and an ever-advancing technology use water for a variety of sometimes conflicting purposes: navigation, flood control, hydropower, irrigation, municipal and industrial water supply, fish and wildlife, and recreation. The corps, in its planning, design, construction, and operating capacities, faces the task of weighing each project and its alternatives, balancing developmental and environmental considerations, and selecting the best solution to meet the needs and aspirations of the public.

Environmental Activities

The passage of the National Environmental Policy Act of 1969 (PL 91–190) strengthened permit authorities (as set forth in Section 13 of the River and Harbor Act of 1899, known as the Refuse Act) for environmental protection. It also provided a firm legal basis for giving due weight to preservation and enhancement of the quality of the environment in connection with the corps' entire program.

The Refuse Act of 1899 makes it illegal to throw, discharge, or deposit refuse matter of any kind or description, other than that flowing from streets and sewers and passing from them in a liquid state, into any navigable waters or their tributaries. On December 23, 1970, the President issued Executive Order 11574, directing that the Secretary of the Army implement a program to administer the Refuse Act. Final regulations were published in the April 7, 1971, edition of the Federal Register. Application forms and a booklet instructing prospective applicants on how to apply for permits were distributed. Those parties currently discharging or depositing material into navigable waters or their tributaries will be required to apply for a permit by July 1, 1971. Parties found to be in violation of the Refuse Act or refusing to comply with the corps' permit program will be referred to the Department of Justice for appropriate legal action.

The regulations require close co-ordination between the Army Corps of Engineers, Environmental Protection Agency (EPA), Department of the Interior, and the National Oceanic and Atmospheric Administration (NOAA). The EPA will advise the corps on the water quality standards applicable to a proposed discharge or deposit and on the impact which the proposed activities may have on water quality considerations. EPA may inform the corps of any limitations or conditions which must be included in any permit, and advise the Department of the Army to deny a permit for reasons relating to water quality.

The Department of the Interior and NOAA will advise the corps of any implications that proposed activities might have on fish and wildlife resources and may recommend that conditions for adequate protection of fish and wildlife be included in the permits granted. The Army's district engineers may deny any application which would have an adverse effect on anchorage or navigation.

The corps is currently developing an automatic data processing program to facilitate the processing of many thousands of permit applications expected by July 1, 1971. The program will be compatible with one being developed by EPA to monitor discharges and water quality in the nation's waterways.

The National Environmental Policy Act of 1969 requires that, with every project recommendation, a statement be submitted detailing the environmental impact, any adverse environmental effects, alternatives to the proposed action, the relationship between man's short-term uses of the environment and the maintenance and enhancement of long-term productivity, and any irreversible or irretrievable commitments of resources which would be involved. An economic, social, and environmental analysis for each possible alternative, including the status quo, must also be indicated. The Corps of Engineers processed to the Council on Environmental Quality 195 draft and 155 final environmental statements as of April 31, 1971. Of these, 120 final environmental impact statements were for authorized civil works projects under construction or in operational status, as well as for permits issued in connection with corps regulatory functions.

In co-operation with the Office of Water Programs, EPA, the corps initiated a pilot wastewater management program to assist state and local agencies in the development of regional wastewater management systems for five of the nine largest urban centers in the United States. San Francisco Bay, Chicago, Cleveland, Detroit, and the Merrimack River Basin north of Boston were selected for early action programs based on expediting ongoing total water management studies of the Army Corps of Engineers. This effort, guided by the principle that pollutants are potential resources out of place, will allow for consideration of the reuse of the beneficial components of wastewater, the immobilization of heavy metals and viruses, and the production of high quality water through wastewater management. The practice of partially treating municipal and industrial discharges still requires the use of U.S.

rivers and lakes to dilute, assimilate, and accumulate chemical and viral wastes. Because many wastes previously not identified as pollutants are now recognized to have significant detrimental effects on the quality of the nation's waters, alternatives to using rivers and lakes as disposal areas for partially treated wastes will be assessed.

In the feasibility studies, each alternative system was evaluated on its ability to meet or exceed federal-state water quality standards. This evaluation also included consideration of pollutants not currently regulated by water quality standards. Subsequent studies will provide a complete analysis of the economic, environmental, and social effects of the more promising alternatives identified in the feasibility studies.

Construction and Management

The fiscal year 1971 appropriation for the Army Corps of Engineers water resources program was $1.310 billion, which covers investigations and surveys, planning, construction, and the operation and maintenance of flood control, river and harbor, beach protection, and hydroelectric projects. Construction activities were performed on 300 specifically authorized navigation, flood control, and multiple purpose projects during the fiscal year.

In 1824 Congress passed the forerunner of the River and Harbor Acts, under which the Corps of Engineers has developed and maintained the nation's waterways for navigation and related purposes. The program now consists of three major elements: coastal harbors and channels, Great Lakes harbors and channels, and inland and intracoastal waterways. To date, the corps has improved in varying degrees some 22,000 miles of inland and intracoastal waterways, a vast majority of which are currently in commercial use. Latest available statistics indicate that foreign and domestic traffic on inland waterways increased 3.9 percent during fiscal year 1971 to establish a new record of 302.9 billion ton-miles.

Nationwide flood control activities were made a function of the Corps of Engineers in 1936. The 1936, 1938, and 1944 Flood Control Acts also assigned to the corps responsibilities for considering and proposing multiple water uses including hydropower, water supply, recreation, and fish and wildlife. Subsequent legislation has expanded the civil works program and added such functions as water quality control and flood plain information service.

Since 1936 the Army Corps of Engineers has completed more than 726 flood control projects. In addition to major reservoir projects, 120 specifically authorized projects were under construction during fiscal year 1971 to provide flood protection to local communities. Many small projects were also constructed under general authorities.

Although the flood control works have performed as intended, other factors, mainly in the acceleration of building and other flood plain encroachments, have led to increasing flood losses. To counter-act this trend the corps is encouraging state and local authorities to adopt flood plain land use regulations. Flood plain information es-sential to regulatory actions has been provided under the Corps Flood Plain Management Services Program for over 1700 locations through-out the nation. Of these areas, 398 have adopted or strengthened land use regulations and 720 more are either studying or in the process of adopting regulations. In addition, some 12,000 corps responses to other requests for flood hazard information is influencing land use at thou-sands of building sites.

Fifty-three projects located in twenty states generate hydroelectric power. At the end of the fiscal year, a total of 12 million kilowatts of generating capacity was in operation, representing 3.8 percent of the total generating capacity of the nation.

Water-oriented recreational activities attract more visitors to corps projects than to any other federal lands. In calendar year 1970 more than 276 million visits were recorded. Typical recreation facilities in-clude tent and trailer sites, picnic areas, boat launching ramps, swim-ming beaches, and sanitary facilities, as well as visitor centers and over-looks. Public use areas of reservoirs are either operated by the corps or leased to states and counties for public park and recreation use.

Construction on the $1.25 billion multiple-purpose McClellan-Kerr Arkansas River Navigation System in Arkansas and Oklahoma was essentially completed in December 1970. The remaining five locks and dams were placed in operation, opening the waterway to Catoosa, Oklahoma, the port facility of Tulsa. Approximately 3 million tons of commodities were transported on the previously completed portion of this navigation project during calendar year 1970. In addition to the navigation feature, the project provides for flood control, hydroelectric power, low-flow regulation and opportunities for water-oriented out-door public recreation.

On January 19, 1971, President Nixon announced the decision to halt construction on the Cross-Florida Barge Canal. The Chief of En-gineers immediately directed the district engineer at Jacksonville to suspend work on all contracts as well as hired labor construction work. Two contracts were subsequently terminated; on March 4 work on the three remaining contracts were reinitiated, with the concurrence of the Council on Environmental Quality, to leave the areas affected by these contracts in a safe condition or to mitigate adverse environ-mental effects. A contract to restore the area of the terminated work to its original condition has been proposed. To implement cessation of work on the project, studies were being conducted by the Department of the Army and the Council on Environmental Quality to develop recommendations for the future of the area.

Measures to insure the safety of structural components of the corps' civil works projects do not end with the successful accomplishment of design and construction. There is a continuing need for periodic surveillance of the behavior and condition of completed structures to insure their structural stability, safety, and operational adequacy, especially when failure or partial failure would endanger human life or cause substantial property damage.

In 1965 the corps established formal procedures for a continuing program of inspection and evaluation of completed structures, as well as for those under construction. Such evaluations, based upon periodic inspections and supported, where appropriate, by programs of instrumentation, are conducted to detect conditions of significant structural distress and to provide a basis for timely initiation of restorative and remedial measures.

Selection priority for establishing inspection programs for completed structures is on the basis of their size and importance and the potential hazard they present. The first general field inspection of newly built structures is carried out immediately after topping out for earth and rockfill dams and embankments, and not later than one year after the project has been placed in service for concrete dams and other structures. Subsequent inspections are scheduled at one- to five-year intervals, depending on the type of structure and its condition at the last inspection.

From 1965 through June 30, 1971, approximately 400 initial inspections and 150 subsequent inspections were conducted on existing major civil works structures. This program made possible early detection of abnormal behavior, which enabled construction of less costly remedial works than if constructed at a later stage of structural deterioration, and averted possible structural failure or partial failure.

Emergency Assistance

The Army Engineers provided disaster assistance in the San Fernando area of California following the February 9, 1971, earthquake. The damaged area extended from the epicenter near Newhall, California, about twenty-six miles southeast through a heavily populated area to the Los Angeles city center. There were 64 people killed and 881 injured. Damage to public and private property was estimated at $436 million.

The Los Angeles district engineer responded immediately to a request from the city of Los Angeles for assistance in rescuing persons trapped in the debris of the Veterans Administration hospital at Sylmar. Under the Corps of Engineers flood fighting authority of Public Law

84–99, water was drained from the severely damaged Lower Van Norman Water Supply Reservoir.

In response to a request from the Office of Emergency Preparedness (OEP) under Public Law 91–606, the corps immediately began a survey of the damaged area. The survey included assessment of damages to utilities: water, power, gas, and sewage. Responding to additional requests from the OEP, the corps provided temporary surface water lines to communities without water, and began repairing and restoring sewer and water lines, streets and sidewalks, and demolishing and removing condemned buildings. As of June 30, 1971, these disaster assistance activities of the Los Angeles Engineer District under PL 91–606 totaled about $10 million.

In February 1971, the Army Corps of Engineers initiated a program (Operation Foresight) of advanced flood emergency operations under PL 84–99 in those areas of the northern states and Alaska having a flood potential due to the above-normal snowpack. Corps personnel placed increased emphasis on observations of flood potential; maintained liaison with other federal, state, and local agencies; and accomplished advanced flood emergency planning including construction of levees, channel clearing, and bank protection, as well as furnishing equipment and supplies. The flood control works constructed under a similar program in 1969 were inspected and, if required, maintenance measures were taken to assure adequate functioning. The total program was accomplished at a cost of $4 million.

Planning

The Army continued its participation in the Federal Water Resources Council's nationwide program of comprehensive river basin regional and framework water and related land resources studies. The Corps of Engineers furnishes members to the interagency co-ordinating committees and commissions established by the council to co-ordinate federal, state, and local planning for comprehensive river basin development. The comprehensive study program consists of nineteen framework studies and twenty-four detailed river basin or regional studies. One framework study has been completed, eleven are in progress, and seven are under consideration. Ten river basin or regional studies have been completed by field-level co-ordinating committees, eight are in progress, and six more are under consideration. The reports submitted by the committees contain recommendations for water and related land resource development to meet the needs of both the near and distant future. As far as specific projects are concerned most of the preauthorization planning is done entirely in the corps, working with the local interests.

As a result of the governmentwide planning, programing, and

budgeting system (PPB), the Army Corps of Engineers adopted a regional approach to multiyear investment planning. The nineteen regions are broken down into 131 river basins, and for each river basin, needs are projected for urban flood damage reduction, rural flood damage reduction, water supply, commercial fisheries, recreation, navigation, and hydroelectric power.

The character and intensity of water resources problems and opportunities vary significantly among the major regions of the nation. Consequently, resource development needs and opportunities must be measured not only in physical terms but also in relation to the region's level of economic development and its concern for environmental restoration or preservation.

During fiscal year 1971, work continued on developing new, improved methodologies to estimate water resource needs in areas of major corps participation: flood control, water supply, navigation, water quality, and recreation. In addition to the work on improvement of needs estimates, attention in fiscal year 1971 was focused on developing a five-year survey program responsive to new and emerging national priorities. In this regard, information is being gathered that will provide a basis for orienting surveys to the resolution of water and related problems for the urban areas of the country. A five-year water resources investment program, reflecting the varying regional requirements, was submitted for consideration by the administration as a basis for selecting new construction and planning starts, and for allocating the funds available for civil works among nineteen major national regions.

The Secretary of the Army submitted his final report on the development of water resources in Appalachia to the Appalachian Regional Commission on April 12, 1971. The report is in response to Section 206 of the Appalachian Regional Development Act of 1965. The commission will submit the report and its views to the President, who will submit it in turn to the Congress.

The recommendations of the secretary are based upon studies made by the Corps Office of Appalachian Studies, with the co-operation of the Water Development Coordinating Committee for Appalachia, through which other federal agencies and the thirteen Appalachian states participated. This landmark effort in comprehensive planning was carried out in the context of inducing economic development in underdeveloped areas. The report recommends ten Corps of Engineers projects, Department of Agriculture upstream watershed and other programs, and a number of TVA (Tennessee Valley Authority) projects.

The Omnibus Rivers and Harbors and Flood Control Acts of 1970 (signed by the President on December 31, 1970) authorize the Corps of Engineers to construct, modify, or otherwise participate in the development of 32 flood control projects, 12 navigation projects, 1 beach erosion control project, and 2 multiple-purpose (including power) projects, all at an estimated federal cost of about $1.270 billion. The acts also include fifty-six sections providing for surveys in the interest of flood control, navigation, and beach erosion control; authorizing modifications to completed projects and changes in existing law; and authorizing special studies of existing projects.

Under the provisions of Section 201 of the 1965 Flood Control Act, the Senate and House Public Works Committees also approved by committee resolutions 28 projects (17 navigation and beach erosion control and 11 flood control), which individually have an estimated federal cost of less than $10 million with a collective total cost of about $395 million.

Civil Works Research and Development

With new directions in the planning and execution of the civil works program and work load, there is an increasing dependence on research to provide timely and practical solutions to water resources management problems. Accordingly, the civil works research and development program has grown significantly in scope and complexity in recent years, and presently encompasses a very broad spectrum of scientific and technical disciplines and interdisciplines in the fields of engineering and construction technology. economics and other social sciences, and ecology and the environment. The program's funding for fiscal year 1971 was about $11 million.

During fiscal year 1971, engineering research continued on construction practices; soils, concrete, and other construction materials; and improvements in site exploration and design techniques to assure more economical construction of locks, dams, levees, floodwalls, and other structures (aiming for greater safety, longer service life, lower operation and maintenance costs, and more flood and earthquake resistance). Efforts are being made to improve the analysis of hydrologic data, with special emphasis on flood control, water supply, pollution abatement, navigation improvement, hydropower, and beach, shore, and riverbank protection.

While civil works research is still oriented primarily toward problems of engineering design, construction technology, and operation and maintenance of completed works, increasing attention is being given to the nonengineering aspects of plan formulation and evaluation, particularly with respect to economics, water quality, and aquatic biology and ecology. In support of the planning effort, the fiscal year 1971 program included research to improve flood plain management and development; economic results of completed projects; recreation design criteria and demand analysis; physical and economic effects of impoundments and releases upon upstream and downstream water quality; water supply economics; economic analysis of requirements for deep-draft harbors; estuarine water quality; aesthetic criteria and evaluation of water resources projects; aquatic plant control studies; and fisheries engineering investigations.

Major increases in research efforts occurred in the biological, ecological, and environmental fields as applicable to coastal waters, reservoir impoundments, construction activities and effects, fish passage facilities at corps projects, and nationwide aquatic plant control. A relatively new field of endeavor for corps research is concerned with the improvement of operation and maintenance techniques. Subjects of research initiated in fiscal year 1971 were the development of better methods for determining depths to which varying densities of material are to be dredged; oil spillage removal; and hydrographic surveying.

The Institute for Water Resources continued to expand its research in social science, economics, and related disciplines, as they apply to the management of the nation's water resources. To improve comprehensive and long-range planning, all social costs and benefits associated with alternative courses of action are explored and evaluated. Concepts and methodologies for consideration of economic, social, environmental, and aesthetic values to be integrated into the planning process are being developed.

Corps field offices propose subjects for research—problems encountered in planning, design, construction, and operation and maintenance of projects. Needs for specific studies in various research areas are determined by the Office of the Chief of Engineers, program requirements are established, and guidance and direction are provided to the research centers or other offices assigned the detailed planning and execution of research projects.

Latest available statistics, compiled in 1968, show that from 1956 to 1965 research expenditures of about $26 million produced directly traceable savings in design, construction, and maintenance costs of about $126 million—approximately a 500 percent return on investment. This estimate is exclusive of less tangible benefits resulting from increased planning, design, and operating reliability, effectiveness, and safety, which are difficult to quantify.

Explosive Excavation

On December 16, 1970, the U.S. Army Engineer Nuclear Cratering Group (NCG) successfully excavated a 400-foot railroad cut with two parallel row shots containing forty-four tons of chemical explosives.

The experiment near the proposed Trinidad Dam on Colorado's Purgatoire River removed about 18,000 cubic yards of sandstone and shale to a depth of 15 to 20 feet with a bottom width of 46 feet. The experiment was part of a project to relocate the Colorado and Wyoming Railroad tracks around the dam site. Two additional railroad relocation experiments are being planned.

To identify suitable project sites for future chemical explosive excavation experiment programs, the Nuclear Cratering Group is evaluating the excavation requirements of about forty corps civil works projects. Project analysis has revealed the need to develop new excavation techniques for sidehill cuts and deep through cuts.

Co-ordination was completed to convert the cratering group to the Explosive Excavation Research Office, an activity of the Waterways Experiment Station, at the end of fiscal year 1971.

Military Engineering

Army engineering efforts are divided into two major functional areas, public works and military engineering. Some activities are common to both fields, and one that has received special attention in both civil and military contexts is the environment. In response to the mandate placed on federal agencies by executive orders, the Army published additional instructions and assigned staff responsibilities for environmental actions. Comprehensive programs were developed to control air and water pollution at Army installations. For the period from fiscal year 1968 through fiscal year 1973, $148 million was programed for air pollution control ($6 million in 1971) and $138 million for water pollution control ($29.5 million in 1971). A program was being developed during the past to control toxic emissions from vehicles, aircraft, and ships.

The Army placed restrictions on the use of certain types of pesticides, revised procurement regulations to implement many new environmental laws and policies, and began research to control noise. The Army won the Department of Defense Conservation Award for 1969, which went to Camp Pickett, Virginia, for outstanding progress in land, forestry, fish, and wildlife management.

The nature of many Army activities requires careful attention to environmental considerations, and environmental impact statements have been required of agencies responsible for a wide variety of programs. Statements that were submitted for review and evaluation included the impact of the Safeguard installations in Montana and North Dakota; the ocean-dumping of chemical munitions; the demilitarization of the chemical and biological munitions at several locations; the transfer of chemical munitions from Okinawa to Johnston Island;

missile testing at White Sands, New Mexico; and a variety of construction projects.

Organization

As part of a continuing program to seek improvements in military engineer troop organizations, a board of officers evaluated contemporary patterns and concepts of nondivisional Army engineer combat units during the year. The objective was to determine the modifications and changes required to provide the most effective combat engineering support within projected force structures, operational plans, and tactical and technical trends. New concepts were developed along with guidance for departmental staff agencies and major commands pertinent to advancement in the combat engineer support field.

A board also studied the structure of the engineer construction battalion, developing alternative organizations that would update requirements and accommodate new equipment and craft skills. Two of the patterns functionalized skills and equipment so that job proficiency could be improved through more effective skill development, utilization, and training. Construction operations of the new units were envisioned to be similar to those of civilian contractors but not identical because of self-defense, unit integrity, and personnel responsibilities peculiar to the armed forces. The two organizational alternatives will be evaluated by the U.S. Army Engineer School and in tests utilizing field troop units.

The new organizational concept for real property maintenance activities support in oversea theaters of operations, outlined in chapter 9, was approved during the year and the Combat Developments Command prepared to implement it. Real property maintenance activities would be transferred from theater Army service support elements to the Theater Army Engineer Command; three new Army engineer organizations—facilities engineering team, group, and district—would be developed and assigned to the Engineer command to provide the real property support.

The roles and assignment of the Theater Army Engineer Command in a theater of operations were also examined and modifications were made to provide a theater commander with a doctrinal base from which to refine the engineer support organization. Requirements for engineer command support were analyzed in the light of theater of operations experience, allocation of resources, priorities of projects, enforcement of standards, massing of support, and provision of technical advice. Adoption of recommended changes would require the engineer command to provide major support in troop construction, contract construction (when designated), real property maintenance, and base topographic support. Even more significant, the engineer command would be assigned to theater Army headquarters rather than a support headquarters to facilitate planning, co-ordination, and control of theaterwide engineer support.

Military Engineering Research and Development

Research in military engineering methods and techniques to support the Army in the field was broadened and increased during the year. New design data for aircraft revetments were developed and disseminated to engineer units in the field. Prototype shelters providing overhead cover were constructed and tested. Thin-walled metal arch structures having a clear span up to eighty feet were included in the program. These structures were designed to support a two-foot-thick layer of concrete or five feet of earth on top of the shell providing protection from direct hits by most artillery, mortar, or rocket projectiles. The structures are sized to shelter existing Army aircraft models.

Research also continued to develop methods of locating covered sources of aggregates (gravels) in delta areas through analysis of various types of aerial and ground contact sensors. As indicated previously, excellent progress has been made to date in special construction materials maps which are being used to aid the highway program in Vietnam.

In conjunction with the Air Force and the Federal Aviation Administration, Army engineers developed permanent pavement design and evaluation criteria applicable to the Air Force C–5A and other multiwheeled and very heavy jumbo aircraft. Development of criteria for expedient pavement surfacing of airfields for such aircraft in theaters of operations was continued. Reports indicate that present design theories and practices are adequate for portland cement concrete pavements, but joints require special care to prevent failure. Previous practices were conservative for asphaltic concrete pavements.

Research was continued to develop methodology for blowing the deck off a bridge by means of an explosion-produced water column. Methods of protecting against this form of bridge demolition were also investigated.

A pre-engineered collapsible and reusable battle-area bunker system which can be emplaced by a squad of men in under eight hours was developed and tested under simulated combat conditions. The system was entirely emplaceable without the use of special tools.

Research and testing was initiated to establish design schemes and construction techniques for protective triggering screens that would detonate incoming shells before they reached a fortification or protective shelter.

Research and testing also continued in nuclear construction engineering under the Corps of Engineers portion of the Army's Nuclear Weapons Effects Research and Test Program. Reports and technical papers on nuclear cratering and on underground and underwater effects of nuclear weapons were published. These reports will be useful in the design and construction of ballistic missile systems and air defense missile employment. A long-range (five-year) Nuclear Weapons Effects Research Plan was published.

Equipment and Bridging

In August 1969, the Army decided to equip construction units with commercial items available off-the-shelf instead of with items designed and manufactured for military use. A pilot program was established to identify cost effectiveness, requirements, types, and characteristics and to evaluate candidate items. Procurement would be based on a standard two-step contract and with a multiyear purchase. At the same time, but as a separate contract, manufacturers would be invited to submit their technical proposals for repair parts support. Firms whose proposals were acceptable would be invited to quote on end items and end item support. Awards would be based on the price of the item package and would consist of two elements: a multiyear contract for commercial construction equipment end items, and an open-end contract for repair parts support. Organizational and maintenance support missions and functions for the commercial items would remain unchanged. Manufacturer's publications would be used for training, operation, maintenance, overhaul, inspection, repair, and parts.

A pilot program covering three items was approved during the fiscal year as follows:

Item	Quantity	Contract Award	Delivery
25-ton crane shovel	240	October 15, 1971	July 15, 1972
1500-gallon asphalt distributor	119	December 31, 1971	August 1, 1972
20-ton dump truck	800	February 13, 1972	September 13, 1972

The Army's ability to cross wet and dry gaps by the use of tactical bridging has been improved. The development of a rapidly erectable floating structure known as the ribbon bridge proceeded to the point of product-testing in swift-running water. It can be easily linked together to form a continuous bridge, or sections may be used for rafts of various sizes and load capacities. The mobility of these units and their speed of assembly permit rapid assault crossing in support of combined arms operations.

Two sets of the medium girder bridge, developed by the British, were procured. When they are delivered early in fiscal year 1972, they will be tested by the Army. These bridges were made of high-strength aluminum alloy components that can be assembled and installed rapidly without the aid of heavy erection equipment. The use of helicopters to emplace the erected bridge is being tested by a joint British-American team.

Mapping and Geodesy

The U.S. Army Topographic Command (TOPOCOM) produced 1,073 new large-scale maps covering 214,600 square miles, and 313 new medium-scale maps covering 1,627,600 square miles during the past year.

TOPOCOM also continued to support the Project MASSTER test facility at Fort Hood. TOPOCOM developed a family of prototype military geographic intelligence products designed to assist battlefield unattended ground sensor activities and to support airmobile operations. These products are being furnished to Project MASSTER for evaluation.

TOPOCOM provided considerable support to NASA with regard to the space program. Work included preparation of Apollo landmark graphics, lunar surface exploration map data packages, simulator models for flight crew training, and a number of lunar topographic maps and photomaps. TOPOCOM also supported the Apollo Hasselblad and lunar topographic camera photography work connected with the topographic evaluation of landing sites and approach corridors for potential Apollo landing sites. Technical and scientific studies were conducted to determine the orientation of a terrain camera in a local lunar co-ordinate system.

TOPOCOM digitized over 150 sheets in the year. Each sheet is a recording on magnetic tape of elevation data at .01-inch intervals. Of the 467 sheets required to cover the continental United States, 302 were complete. The Electromagnetic Compatibility Analysis Center is the primary user of the digital terrain data produced by TOPOCOM.

During May 1971 TOPOCOM produced a special block of digital terrain data covering a fire base area in Southeast Asia. These data are being used by the Army Materiel Systems Analysis Agency to prepare a scenario of the operations in the fire base area. This scenario is to support the Army position of rotary-wing air support versus the Air Force's fixed-wing air support. The subject was being considered by the Packard Committee as the year closed.

TOPOCOM continued to support Department of Defense requirements for more precise determination of horizontal and vertical control for specific locations on the surface of the earth.

Among major ground survey projects, the TOPOCOM completed a 600-mile traverse, accomplished by electro-optical means to one part per million accuracy, along the coast of California. Ties from this line were made to coastal islands as well as across the San Andreas Fault to a National Ocean Survey precise traverse. Surveys in support of mapping were completed in Iran. Control survey support to gravity surveys was provided in New Mexico, Florida, Wisconsin, and Mexico. Continuing survey support was provided at the White Sands Missile Range as well as at the Arizona Test Range. Parties were fielded to establish astronomic positions at missile sites.

The trend toward satellite geodesy continued at an accelerated pace with TOPOCOM receiving four sets of Doppler receiver equipment during fiscal year 1971. Doppler-derived positions were obtained for sites in Turkey, the Falklands, Chile, Argentina, the Pacific, and Scandinavia, as well as for a number of U.S. sites. Participation in BC–4 optical satellite tracking was phased out.

The Department of Defense requirement for worldwide gravity coverage continued to be a top survey priority. In the United States, gravity surveys were completed by TOPOCOM in California, Florida, and West Virginia. Work continued in Arizona, New Mexico, Missouri, Wisconsin, and Michigan. Major survey areas outside the United States are Mexico, Iceland, Norway, and Finland, where TOPOCOM and the host countries are conducting co-operative surveys. A gravity survey of the near-shore waters of Norway was continued during the summer months, and underwater surveys in some U.S. waters were completed. Final tests of the Helicopter Gravity Measuring System were completed and the data were being evaluated as the year closed.

XII. Special Functions

Administration of the Ryukyu Islands

The United States continued during fiscal year 1971 to administer the Ryukyu Islands, under the provisions of Article 3 of the Treaty of Peace with Japan; the largest island of the Ryukyuan archipelago is Okinawa, where the United States maintains a large military base. The responsibility for governing this area had been assigned by the President to the Secretary of Defense, who further delegated it to the Department of the Army. The agency which carries out this responsibility in the field is the U.S. Civil Administration of the Ryukyu Islands (USCAR), which is headed by a high commissioner appointed by the Secretary of Defense with the concurrence of the Secretary of State and the President's approval. An indigenous government exercises broad legislative, executive, and judicial authority in performing day-to-day governmental functions, under the leadership of an elected legislature and chief executive.

Negotiations between the United States and Japan, which had been initiated in April 1970 to prepare the Reversion Agreement pursuant to the Nixon-Sato understanding of November 1969, continued at an intensive pace throughout most of this period. These negotiations culminated in the signing of the agreement on June 17, 1971, by Secretary of State William P. Rogers and Japanese Foreign Minister Kiichi Aichi—the former in Washington and the latter in Tokyo. The simultaneous ceremony was given extensive television coverage, via satellite, throughout Japan, Okinawa, and the United States. Following the signing of the agreement itself, a number of related agreements were signed or initialed in Tokyo by U.S. Ambassador Armin H. Meyer and Foreign Minister Aichi.

As the reporting period closed, preparations were being made to submit the agreement to the U.S. Senate for advice and consent, and to the Japanese Diet for its approval. After it receives the necessary legislative support in both countries, ratifications will be exchanged on a mutually agreed date, and reversion will take place two months thereafter. The agreement is believed to be a reasonable compromise between the objectives sought by the two countries, and its eventual enactment will be an important milestone in furthering U.S.-Japanese relations.

Although reversion will mean that the responsibility for governing the Ryukyus will be returned to Japan, it will by no means result in the abandonment of the U.S. base on Okinawa, which has provided major support during both the Korean War and the present conflict in Vietnam. The Okinawa base will be maintained after reversion, when it will be subject to the same arrangements that now apply to U.S. military forces in Japan under the 1960 Treaty of Mutual Cooperation and Security.

While the Army is about to lay aside its responsibility for governing the Ryukyus, it has not lessened its efforts to furthur the economic and social advancement of the Ryukyuan people, which continued during fiscal year 1971 with a rise of the per capita income to an all-time high of $770, 18.2 percent over that of the previous year. Private consumption expenditures continued to rise, reflecting the upward surge in the Ryukyuan economy. Confidence in its continued strength was revealed by a 14.3 percent increase in private investment by Ryukyuans and foreigners. Although the Ryukyuan balance of trade continued to show a wide disparity between imports and exports, the gap was greatly offset by U.S. expenditures, estimated at $329 million. The largest part of this total ($221 million) came from local base expenditures. There were also U.S. grants and loans amounting to $33 million ($12 million in appropriated aid, $19 million from the USCAR General Fund, and $2 million of aid in kind). The balance came from U.S. investments of $48 million and Ryukyuan exports in the amount of $27 million to the United States.

Although U.S. administrative rights in the Ryukyus will remain intact and unimpaired until the time of reversion, continuing efforts were made during the reporting period to prepare for a smooth transfer of governmental functions to Japan. The U.S.-Japan Preparatory Commission (established in Naha pursuant to the 1969 Nixon-Sato understanding) worked out a number of important arrangements whereby USCAR would progressively disengage from a number of governmental functions, even before reversion. Thus Japan will gradually take over the task of providing advice and assistance to the government of the Ryukyu Islands, of supervising the administration of Japan's own economic aid program, and of restructuring certain Ryukyuan social and economic institutions to conform to those in Japan.

The Okinawan economy is thriving, and the destruction caused by the last great Pacific military campaign has been erased from the landscape. Many public utilities, hitherto virtually unknown, have been developed with American funds. An area that was once predominantly agricultural has undergone an economic revolution, and an emerging industrial and commercial society has evolved. The standard of living now is at an all-time high, being exceeded in all of Asia only by that of Japan itself.

Administration of the Panama Canal

By authority delegated to him as the personal representative of the President, the Secretary of the Army has special responsibilities for Panama Canal matters which include operations of the Canal Zone government and Panama Canal Company. The Canal Zone government is administered under the supervision of the Secretary of the Army by the governor of the Canal Zone who is appointed by the President. Management of the Panama Canal Company is vested in a board of directors appointed by the Secretary of the Army as "stockholder," representing the interests of the United States as owner of the corporation. The Secretary of the Army has appointed the Under Secretary of the Army as a member and the chairman of the board.

In fiscal year 1971, 14,617 oceangoing ships, including 503 United States government vessels, passed through the canal. Toll revenues were approximately $97 million, which included credits for transits of United States government vessels. Panama Canal revenues are applied against operating and capital expenses of the canal enterprise. Detailed financial statements are published in the annual reports of the Panama Canal Company and Canal Zone government. The toll figure for 1971 represented a decrease of approximately $4 million from 1970.

Interoceanic Canal Studies

Determining the feasibility of building a new sea-level canal to accommodate the increasing number of ships desiring to use such a waterway was the task of the Atlantic-Pacific Interoceanic Canal Study Commission. This commission terminated its five-year study and forwarded its report to the President on November 30, 1970. The Department of the Army represented the Department of Defense on this presidential commission, with the Chief of Engineers acting as the engineering agent for the commission and directing the engineering feasibility portion of the study. The Deputy Under Secretary of the Army (International Affairs) chaired a study group which prepared the Defense annex to the commission's report.

With the submission of its final report, the Atlantic-Pacific Interoceanic Canal Study Commission terminated its work and closed its offices. The President directed that the Secretaries of State and the Army would be jointly responsible for handling future queries and correspondence of the commission—the Secretary of State in regard to foreign policy questions and the Secretary of the Army in other matters. Within the Department of the Army, this new responsibility was assigned to the Office of the Deputy Under Secretary of the Army (International Affairs).

Promotion of Rifle Practice

A reorientation of the Civilian Marksmanship Program was completed during fiscal year 1971 and the number of clubs supported by the National Board for the Promotion of Rifle Practice (NBPRP) appeared to have stabilized. On June 30, 1970, 3,183 clubs and 192,172 individual members were supported by the program. By December 31, 1970, these figures had declined to 3,093 clubs and 185,494 individuals. Some fifty clubs were awaiting enrollment, and by the end of the fiscal year the totals were little changed from 1970.

Under the Civilian Marksmanship Program, 300 rounds of caliber-.22 ammunition are issued to eligible members of newly enrolled junior rifle clubs for each of the first two years of affiliation, followed by free issues based upon availability of resources. Ammunition may be purchased by clubs at any time. Newly affiliated clubs are also issued .22-caliber rifles on indefinite loan.

Appropriated funds to support this program in fiscal year 1971 were increased to $102,000. The program could thus be supported at the level authorized by Army regulations.

In 1970, as in previous years, the National Board for the Promotion of Rifle Practice granted authority to the National Rifle Association of America to conduct four of the five National Trophy Matches at the 1970 NRA National Championships at Camp Perry, Ohio. A total of sixty teams, including thirty-two civilian teams, and 1,114 individuals competed for service rifle and service pistol trophies and medals in the NBPRP National Trophy Matches. Since 1967, due to budgetary considerations and operational requirements involving Southeast Asia, the decision to provide Army support for the National Matches has been made on an annual basis.

During the past year 300 National Match .30-caliber M1 rifles were authorized for sale to competitive high power rifle shooters, representing a return to the U.S. Treasury of $46,000.

XIII. Summary

Despite American disengagement from Southeast Asia, the Vietnam War remained the dominant factor in Army affairs in fiscal year 1971. The effects extended into all functional areas, and the Army had to deal not only with the details of the ongoing conflict, but with a variety of future actions induced by the war.

Casualties were sharply reduced as a result of the shift from a fighting to a holding posture, and replacement needs declined as more troops and units were redeployed. Draft calls dropped, the training base was contracted, and the over-all size of the Army was reduced. The central problem was to accomplish the cutback while maintaining an effective fighting force to carry forward continuing battlefield responsibilities and meet commitments at home and around the world. The size, form, and capability of the postwar Army also had to be kept constantly in view and carefully geared to ongoing actions.

The withdrawal from Southeast Asia created a logistical challenge of the first magnitude. By the year's close, good progress had been made in redistributing some of the huge stocks of supplies and equipment and in transferring some of the installations and facilities no longer required by American forces. The Vietnamese forces, the U.S. Military Assistance Program, and the Reserve Components were the beneficiaries of the reducing American commitment and the increasing availability of materiel.

Social problems raised or heightened by the war became increasingly visible during the year, and new approaches were undertaken to solve them. Numerous co-ordinated actions were in progress to attract volunteers to Army service and eliminate dependence upon the draft, and by year's end there were promising signs as volunteers were being enlisted despite reduced draft pressures.

Clearly, fiscal year 1972 would be a critical period. The modern volunteer army would have to progress at a time when national priorities were being reordered and resources reallocated. The Army would continue to operate under conditions of declining strength, a shrinking support base, a lingering war, and reduced appropriations.

Index

www.ingramcontent.com/pod-product-compliance
Lightning Source LLC
Chambersburg PA
CBHW021337090426
42742CB00008B/632